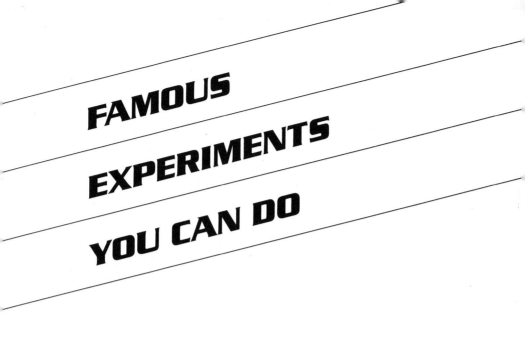

FAMOUS
EXPERIMENTS
YOU CAN DO

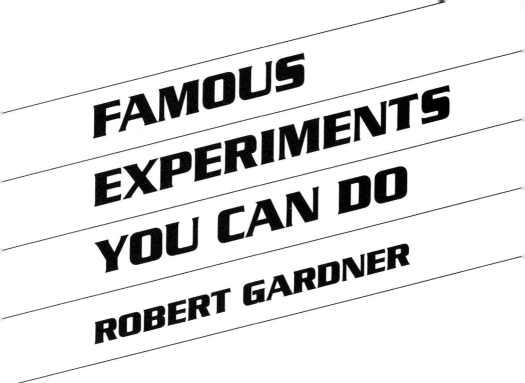

FAMOUS
EXPERIMENTS
YOU CAN DO
ROBERT GARDNER

AN EXPERIMENTAL
SCIENCE SERIES BOOK

FRANKLIN WATTS
NEW YORK/LONDON
TORONTO/SYDNEY/1990

Photographs courtesy of: Brown Brothers: pp. 27, 69, 124, 130;
The Bettmann Archive: pp. 48, 100;
New York Public Library, Picture Collection: pp. 92, 114, 120.

Library of Congress Cataloging-in-Publication Data

Gardner, Robert, 1929-

Famous experiments you can do / Robert Gardner.
    p. cm. — (An Experimental science series book)
Contents: Includes bibliographical references.
Summary: Demonstrates scientific principles in the fields of chemistry and physics by replicating experiments performed by such scientists as Archimedes, Galileo, Antoine Lavoisier, and Sir Isaac Newton.
ISBN 0-531-10883-X
1. Physics—Experiments—Juvenile literature. 2. Chemistry, Physical
and theoretical—Experiments—Juvenile literature.
[1. Physics—Experiments. 2. Chemistry—Experiments.
3. Experiments.] I. Title. II. Series.
QC25.G37   1990
530'.078—dc20   CIP   AC

CONTENTS

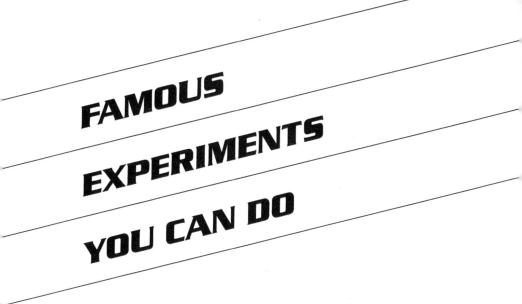

FAMOUS
EXPERIMENTS
YOU CAN DO

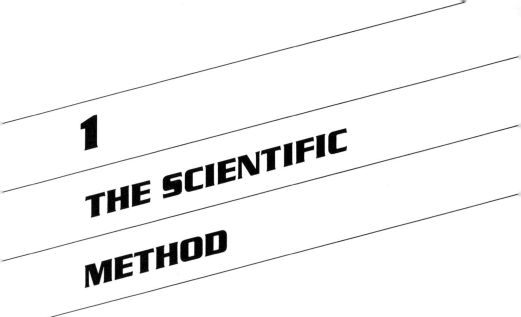

1
THE SCIENTIFIC
METHOD

Science began when early humans noticed and recorded the recurrent cycles that filled their lives. They observed, on a daily basis, the way sunset was followed by darkness until the sun emerged again on the opposite horizon, passed across the sky, and set once more. On a monthly basis, they saw the moon wax from crescent to first quarter to full, only to wane again to third quarter, crescent, and finally disappear.

As years passed, they noticed that seasonal changes were accompanied by changes in the constellations that crossed the night sky. As the visible stars that dotted the heavens changed, the sun's east to west path across the daytime sky moved slowly northward, then southward, then northward again. They noticed also that the sun and the moon were not the only heavenly bodies that wandered among the stars. Certain bright bodies that looked like stars seemed to slowly change their positions among the predominantly fixed stars that filled most of the night sky.

We know today that these "wanderers" were the planets Mercury, Venus, Mars, Jupiter, and Saturn. The days of the week were named for these wanderers, the sun, and the moon. Monday was named for the moon, Tuesday for Mars, Wednesday for Mercury, Thursday for Jupiter, and Friday for Venus. You can easily determine the days of the week named for the sun and Saturn.

As long ago as 2000 B.C., Babylonians kept careful records of the rising and setting times of Venus before and after sunset. By the fifth century B.C., astronomers had learned through careful observations to predict the eclipses of the sun and moon. Views through the carefully aligned giant stones at Stonehenge, England, on June 21 make it clear that the Druids, or whoever built Stonehenge a few centuries before the birth of Christ, were not only aware of changes in the sun's path across the heavens, but had carefully marked the position of sunrise at summer solstice as well.

DEDUCTIVE VS. INDUCTIVE REASONING

Though careful observations of the sun, moon, and stars enabled early humans to make astronomical predictions, the rise of modern science did not begin until the seventeenth century. The great philosophers of Greece—Socrates, Plato, and Aristotle—were brilliant people, capable of superb reasoning, who believed there was a universal and absolute truth that humans could discover through pure reason. However, their approach was entirely deductive; that is, they reasoned from what they thought were self-evident premises. For example, consider the following syllogisms:

All men are good. Socrates is a man.
Therefore, Socrates is good.
$X > Y$; $Y > Z$; therefore, $X > Z$.

The reasoning in these examples is perfectly clear and straightforward. But suppose the premise from which the reasoning stems is wrong. In the first syllogism we must assume that *all* men are good; that is the premise. A brief study of history and a reading of the daily newspaper will soon convince you that such a premise is false. Clearly, reasoning based on a false premise can lead to false conclusions.

Modern science seeks to establish the truth of the premises from which deductive reasoning starts. Although it was not until the seventeenth century that such attempts were made by a significant number of people, there were a few rare individuals who used what we would call scientific reasoning before that time. The style of Leonardo da Vinci (1452–1519) would certainly be characterized as scientific. He recognized that details are important and that we cannot understand nature or solve problems solely by reasoning from general principles. His studies led him to realize the falseness of many of the established principles about nature, which were based on the works of Aristotle and other early Greek philosophers. He believed that the way to understand nature was through inductive reasoning (using specific facts to formulate general principles) and that generalizations about nature could be discovered by finding common threads among a large number of specific examples. Given enough facts and observations, we may find a common principle that unifies and explains all the specific details. It was Leonardo who said,

> Those sciences are vain and full of errors which are not born from experiment, the mother of all certainty, and which do not end with one clear experiment.

Although Leonardo was correct in recognizing the important role of experimentation in seeking to understand nature, he was wrong in assuming that it is the "mother of all certainty." There may well be exceptions to any generalization based on specific facts, observations, events, and data no one has analyzed. We can never analyze every fact related to the generalization nor anticipate each and every consequence that may emerge from a general principle. The test of any general principle lies in our ability to use that principle to make predictions about the natural world that can then be checked by experiment. As a principle survives more and more tests of its validity, we become increasingly confident that it is true, but we never reach the point of absolute certainty because there is always the possibility that an exception may be found.

ATOMISTS VS. CONTINUISTS

Over the past 400 years the method of scientific inquiry has enabled us to settle the philosophical differences that emerged between two groups of thinkers in ancient Greece, known as the atomists.

and the continuists. The atomists, exemplified by Democritus, believed that matter consisted of atoms. They argued that if we tried to break matter into smaller and smaller pieces, eventually we would reach a point where the matter could no longer be divided. This smallest piece of matter would be the atom of which everything was made. Between the atoms was nothing—the void.

The continuists, led by Aristotle, believed that all matter was made of the same stuff—hyle—which completely filled space. Hyle could be modified into the four elements of fire, earth, air, and water. Earth was at the center of all matter surrounded by shells of water, air, and fire. Heavy matter, such as earth, lay below lighter matter, such as water. Fire, because it was the lightest, lay above all the others. Heavy objects, such as stones, fell toward the earth because that was the natural place for heavy matter.

Although the philosophy of Aristotle dominated Western thought prior to the seventeenth century, we know now that the atomists were closer to the truth about matter than the continuists. However, both philosophies were based on speculation and common sense. Neither group could support its point of view with concrete evidence. In fact, the idea of designing experiments to test the consequences of their theories never occurred to them.

THE AGE OF SCIENCE

Individual scientists such as Leonardo da Vinci and Nicholas Copernicus (1473–1543) used sound scientific procedures, but it was not until the seventeenth century that groups of people who engaged in what we would call science began to meet, share ideas, and form professional organizations. It was early in that century that the Accadèmia dei Lincei and the Accadèmia del Cimento arose in Italy. The Royal Society was chartered in England in 1662 and the Académie des Sciences was founded in Paris in 1666 during the reign of Louis XIV. Such organizations allowed scientists to share knowledge, to critique one another's work or ideas, and to gain confidence in this new method of seeking to understand nature's ways.

The newly organized societies enabled scientists to share the fundamental tools of science that were being developed at that time—the microscope, telescope, thermometer, barometer, air pump, and pendulum clock. These were used by the new breed of natural philosophers to seek and find some of nature's unifying principles and regularities.

In this book we will examine some of the great experiments conducted by early scientists, experiments that changed the course of history. You will have the opportunity to repeat some of these experiments. For example, you can record the rising and setting time of Venus before and after sunset, just as the Babylonians did. It's not hard to locate Venus. It's the brightest "wanderer" in the sky. When it's visible, it appears in the eastern sky before sunrise or in the western sky after sunset.

If you watch Venus, record its rising and setting times relative to sunrise and sunset, and measure the angle between Venus and the sun, perhaps you will discover the same patterns that the early Babylonians noticed. If you decide to make these observations, **never look directly at the sun. The sun can cause permanent damage to your eyes.**

You can watch the sun and moon, too, record their positions, map their paths, and find the same regularities discovered by early astronomers. But it will take considerable time to find these patterns, for you cannot change the time frame of the heavens. As you wait and watch, you'll have time to discover other patterns, regularities, and principles of nature that can be uncovered in much less time. You can follow procedures that are the same as, or similar to, those that Galileo, Newton, Faraday, Pasteur, and other great scientists used in arriving at the basic principles of nature. Your discoveries will not be as original as theirs, but you can share the same excitement of discovery that they experienced.

The investigations found in this book were chosen for several reasons. First, they were significant in the development of scientific thought. Often they represented breakthroughs in our attempts to comprehend the enigmas of nature. Second, they can be done with relatively simple equipment that you can generally find in your home or school. And third, you do not have to be an expert in physics, chemistry, medicine, or botany in order to understand how to do the experiments or interpret the results.

2

EUREKA! IT'S ARCHIMEDES

Although Archimedes lived long before the modern Scientific Revolution, his approach to solving problems through experimentation was 1,800 years ahead of his contemporaries. However, like the early Greek philosophers who preceded him, he regarded learning by experimenting as inferior to the brilliant geometric deductive thinking for which he is also famous.

ARCHIMEDES (287–212 B.C.)

There are more anecdotes about Archimedes than perhaps any other scientist in history. The one that is best known tells of Archimedes moving about in his bathtub contemplating a problem that the king, Hiero II, had asked him to solve. According to the legend, Hiero had asked Archimedes to find out whether a crown made for him by a goldsmith was really pure gold as he had requested. The king suspected the goldsmith had used a less precious metal such as silver to form the crown and had then covered it with gold. Of course, the king did not want to destroy his expensive crown to check his suspicions, so he requested Archimedes to answer his question without damaging the crown.

As he lowered more of his body into the bath, Archimedes noticed that the level of the water in the tub rose. When he lifted more of his body above the surface, the water level fell. Suddenly, in a flash, he saw the answer. He leaped from the tub and, completely naked, ran through the streets of Syracuse, Sicily, shouting, "Eureka! Eureka!" (Eureka means "I've got it!")

Suddenly seeing a solution to a problem is not uncommon among scientists. Thinking about a problem off and on seems to generate subconscious mental activity that may provide an insight or a new configuration of ideas that leads to a solution. Once the solution appears, it may seem so obvious and simple that one wonders why it took so long to solve the problem.

According to this particular legend, Archimedes suddenly realized that the volume of an irregularly shaped body could be measured by placing it in water. The body's volume would displace an equal volume of water. Archimedes could then weigh the crown, determine its density (mass per volume), and compare the density of the crown with the density of gold. Gold is denser than silver, hence it displaces less water than an equal mass of silver.

Archimedes' solution to a practical problem was useful to King Hiero, who learned that the goldsmith had indeed cheated him, but, more importantly, it started Archimedes on a series of experiments that led to an understanding of a general scientific principle that you, too, can discover.

INVESTIGATION 1: ARCHIMEDES' DISCOVERY
To begin, weigh a fairly large piece of metal such as a lead sinker, a metal cylinder, a stack of coins, or something similar to one of these. Then find the volume of the metal sample you have chosen. If it has a regular shape, such as a cylinder or a cube, you can find the volume by measuring its dimensions and multiplying the area of its base by its height. If its shape is irregular, you can find the volume by immersing it in some water in a graduated cylinder or measuring cup and seeing how much the water level rises. If the object is too large to fit into a measuring cup, you can use an overflow can. (This is the method Archimedes used with the crown.) Next, weigh a volume of water equal to the volume displaced by the metal. Then weigh the piece of metal while submerged in water, as shown in figure 1.

How does the metal's weight when submerged compare with its weight in air? How does the metal's loss of weight in water compare with the weight of the water it displaces?

Repeat the experiment several times using different metals and different liquids (try rubbing alcohol and/or witch hazel) as well as water. Within the accuracy of your measurements, does the metal's loss of weight in the liquid always equal the weight of the liquid displaced?

INVESTIGATION 2: MOVING THE EARTH
It was Archimedes who said, "Give me a place to stand and I can move the earth." His statement

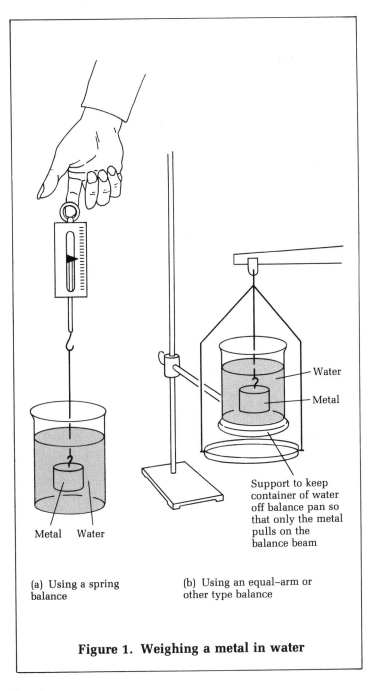

Water

Metal

Support to keep
container of water
off balance pan so
that only the metal
pulls on the
balance beam

Metal   Water

(a) Using a spring
balance

(b) Using an equal–arm or
other type balance

Figure 1. Weighing a metal in water

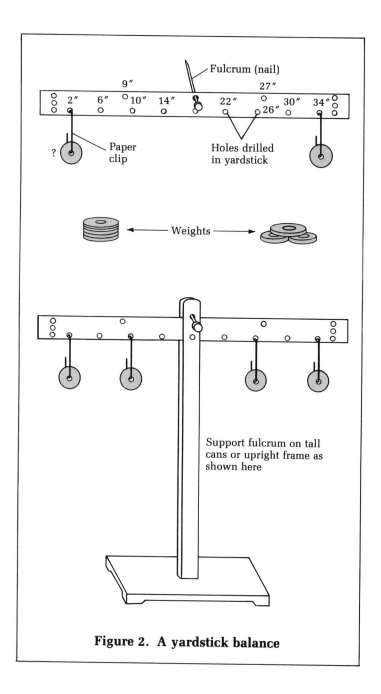

Figure 2. A yardstick balance

was based on the principle of the lever, which he had discovered. To find this principle for yourself, as Archimedes might have done, take a yardstick and make it into a simple balance. **Ask an adult to help you drill holes** in it. (See figure 2.) Support the balance with a nail at the top, center hole.

Using weights or heavy identical washers, hang a known weight from a paper clip or a piece of string at, say, 16 inches to the right of the balance's center. (The point from which the balance is supported, in this case, the center, is called the fulcrum or axis.) What weight is required at 16 inches to the left of the fulcrum to balance the weight on the right, that is, to make the balance beam level? Leaving the right side of the balance unchanged, what weight is required on the left side to balance the beam if the weight there is placed 8 inches from the fulcrum? Four inches from the fulcrum?

Try a variety of weights and distances and record the weights and positions required for balance in each case. Can you find a principle or rule that enables you to predict all conditions where balance will be achieved?

Now place the nail which serves as a fulcrum so that it is no longer in the center, but rather 9 inches from one end of the beam. As you can see, the beam is not level because the weight of the beam is no longer equally distributed. Does the beam rotate in the direction you would expect it to turn? To make the beam level, place some clay on the light side of the beam, or tape washers or some other object to it. If you are to use the least amount of clay or washers, where on the beam should you place this counterweight?

With the beam in balance again, see if your principle still works. What weight placed 8 inches from the fulcrum on the short side of the beam will balance 100 grams (or two washers) placed 16 inches from the fulcrum on the long side of the balance? Try other weights and positions with this unequal-length beam to test your rule. Does the rule always work?

Use your principle to explain what force (in pounds) the person in figure 3a would have to exert on the crowbar to lift the 500-pound stone. What force would the fisherman in figure 3b have to exert to lift the 10-pound fish? What did Archimedes mean when he said he could move the earth if given a place to stand?

CHALLENGES FROM ARCHIMEDES

1. Extend Archimedes' principle to bodies that float as well as those that sink. How can you tell from a floating body's density what fraction of the body will sink?

2. Design an object that will neither float nor sink but remain suspended in the middle of a liquid.

3. Archimedes extended his discovery to all fluids (gases as well as liquids) by showing that a body placed in a fluid is buoyed upward by a force equal to the weight of the fluid displaced. To demonstrate that this is true for a body weighed in a gas as well as one weighed in a liquid, weigh a collapsed, empty plastic bag. Then fill the bag with air and weigh it again. What do you find? Try to explain your results in terms of Archimedes' principle.

Carbon dioxide has a density of about 1.8

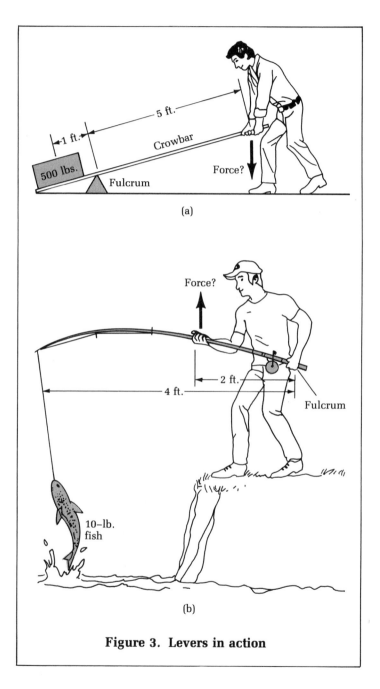

(a)

(b)

Figure 3. Levers in action

grams per liter at room temperature and normal air pressure. How much do you think a liter of carbon dioxide would weigh in air, which has a density of about 1.2 grams per liter under the same conditions? Design and carry out an experiment to test your prediction.

4. You might repeat Archimedes' actual experiment more closely if you weighed a gold object in air and then in water. Unfortunately, most people cannot afford gold crowns, so you would have to use something small, like a gold ring. What problems would this present?

5. Many people do possess silver objects that are reasonably large. Use Archimedes' experiment to find out if a large object such as a set of silver spoons are really pure silver. (The density of pure silver is 10.5 grams per cubic centimeter.)

6. Referring to figure 2, suppose you place the fulcrum nail through the center hole or the bottom hole at the 18-inch position. What happens to the stability of the beam under each of these conditions? Can you explain why?

ERATOSTHENES (276–196 B.C.)

While the brilliance of Archimedes shone in Sicily, a Greek astronomer named Eratosthenes quietly found a way to measure the size of the earth. In Syene, a city 500 miles south of Alexandria where Eratosthenes lived, people could see the sun's image reflected in a deep well at midday on the date marking the summer solstice (June 21). Eratosthenes realized that such an observation meant that the sun must be directly overhead in Syene at that time. He decided to measure the shadow of a

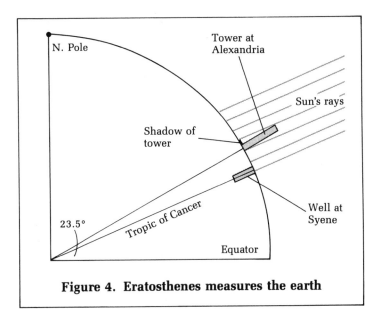

Figure 4. Eratosthenes measures the earth

tall vertical tower in Alexandria at midday on the same day that the sun was directly overhead in Syene. His measurements revealed that at midday the tower cast a shadow 6.6 feet long, a ratio of shadow length to tower height of about 0.13. With all this information, and assuming the light from the sun to be parallel beams because of the sun's great distance from the earth, Eratosthenes calculated the earth's circumference and diameter.

INVESTIGATION 3:
THE SIZE OF THE EARTH
Using Eratosthenes' data and assumption as well as figure 4, calculate the earth's circumference and diameter. What values do you get? The figure that Eratosthenes obtained seemed too large to most people of his time, and they ignored his findings, which were quite accurate.

3
GALILEO, HARVEY, AND REDI

Galileo's realization that experimentation and mathematics, not blind adherence to the teaching of the ancients, were the keys to unlocking nature's secrets marked the beginning of what might be called modern science.

GALILEO GALILEI (1564–1642)

Although his last name was Galilei, this scientist is always referred to by his first name. It was Galileo who brought science back to the quantitative method that Archimedes had pioneered 1,800 years before. Galileo's discoveries in science are many, and he may rightly be regarded as the father of modern science.

One of his earliest discoveries, while he was still a student at the University of Pisa, occurred one morning when he was attending church. Unable to concentrate on the sermon, he watched a chandelier, driven by varying air currents,

Galileo Galilei (1564–1642) is regarded by many
as the "father of modern science." He was forced by
the Inquisition to renounce the Copernican system
of planetary motion and to abandon his studies.

swing through arcs of different lengths. Using his pulse as a timing device, he thought that the time it took the chandelier to swing back and forth was independent of the arc through which it moved. When he returned from church, he began an investigation of the pendulum. You can carry out the same experiments that he did. However, you may prefer to use a stopwatch rather than your pulse to time events. Galileo had no choice— there were no mechanical devices in the sixteenth century to measure short time intervals.

INVESTIGATION 4:
THE PENDULUM
To make a pendulum, clamp two pieces of wood firmly together to suspend a long string that has a pendulum bob on its lower end. The pendulum can be shortened or lengthened by pulling the string between the wooden clamps when they are loosened. (See figure 5.) Attach the suspension for the pendulum to a table, the top of a door frame, or some other place where the pendulum can swing freely.

If you use relatively light bobs, a long piece of thread suspended from a thumbtack stuck in the top of a door frame will do.

Half the distance the pendulum bob swings (from the end to the middle) is called the amplitude of the swing. By measuring the period of a pendulum (the time to make one complete swing, over and back), you can check up on Galileo's idea that the period is independent of the amplitude. Why will it be more accurate to measure the time it takes to make 50 or 100 complete swings (over and back) rather than just one?

Begin by making a pendulum about a meter

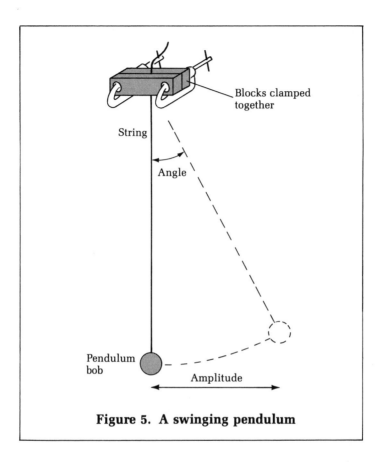

Figure 5. A swinging pendulum

long. A weight with a hook on it or a heavy washer can be used as a bob. Pull the bob out so that the pendulum swings through an angle of about 30 degrees. Determine the time it takes to make 50 or 100 complete swings. Divide that total time by the number of swings to find the period (the time to make one swing). Repeat the experiment, but this time have the pendulum swing through an angle of only 5 or 10 degrees. Was Galileo right?

Does the period of the pendulum change as it swings? How do you know?

Galileo continued to work with pendulums and investigated a number of other variables experimentally. You can carry out the same experiments that he did. For example, how does the weight of the bob affect the period of the pendulum? To find out, you can vary the weight of the bob and measure the period as before. You can use two washers instead of one, or use a 200-gram weight instead of 100 grams. To be sure that the length of the pendulum does not change, always measure the length of the pendulum from the point of support (where the string is clamped) to the center of the weight. How does the weight of the bob affect the period of the pendulum?

Does the length of a pendulum affect its period? Does the period double when the length doubles? To find out how the period of a pendulum is related to its length, measure the period when the pendulum's length is 0.25 m, 0.50 m, 0.75 m, 1.00 m, 1.50 m, and, if possible, 2.00 m. Galileo found that the period of a pendulum when squared was proportional to its length; that is,

$$T^2 = kL,$$

where T is the period, L is the length, and k is a proportionality constant.

To find out if your results agree with Galileo's, plot a graph of the pendulum's period squared (T^2) as a function of its length (L); that is, plot T^2 on the vertical axis and L on the horizontal axis. Do the points of your graph lie very close to a straight line? If so, what do you conclude?

What is the slope (rise/run) of your graph?
What is the significance of the slope?

THE STARRY MESSENGER
In his introduction to *The Starry Messenger* in
1610, Galileo wrote:

> *It is a very beautiful thing, and most grat-*
> *ifying to the sight, to behold the body of*
> *the moon, distant from us almost sixty*
> *earthly diameters [this should have been*
> *radii, but Galileo wrote diameters] as if it*
> *were no farther away than two such*
> *measures—so that its diameter appears*
> *almost thirty times larger, its surface*
> *nearly nine hundred times, and its vol-*
> *ume twenty-seven thousand times as*
> *large as when viewed with the naked eye.*
> *In this way, one may learn with all the*
> *certainty of sense evidence that the moon*
> *is not robed in a smooth and polished sur-*
> *face but is in fact rough and uneven, cov-*
> *ered everywhere, just like the earth's sur-*
> *face, with huge prominences, deep val-*
> *leys, and chasms.*

What Galileo saw when he viewed the moon with
the help of a telescope startled him more than it
will you when you look at the same body. The
Greeks believed that the celestial bodies were
perfect, that the moon and sun and all the stars
were perfectly spherical bodies following perfectly circular orbits about the earth. Galileo saw the
imperfections of the moon with his own eyes. He
knew the Greeks had been wrong. If they were

[31]

wrong about the moon, perhaps they had formulated other falsehoods as well.

So strongly did people believe in the perfect nature of celestial bodies that many attacked Galileo, saying that he was being fooled because the telescope through which he gazed distorted the sense of sight. They said the same about the eyesight of those who viewed the supernova that suddenly appeared in the heavens in the year 1604.

The German astronomer and mystic Johannes Kepler had written to Galileo asking him to support the "Copernican model." Named for the Polish astronomer Nicholas Copernicus, the Copernican theory held that the sun, which was motionless, was the center of the solar system and that the planets, including the earth, revolved around it. But Galileo had refused. Then, after observing through his telescope the moons of Jupiter circling that planet, Galileo realized that there was nothing sacred about the earth. If moons could circle Jupiter, why should not the earth circle the sun?

INVESTIGATION 5:
VIEWS THROUGH A
TELESCOPE OR BINOCULARS
To see the craters and valleys of the moon as Galileo saw them, turn a telescope or a good pair of binoculars on the moon, preferably during its early or late phases when the shadows of the lunar mountains will be longest. Of course, it will be best if you can examine the moon frequently as it changes from a new crescent moon through all its phases to its final crescent just before it slips between the sun and the earth. You will see clearly that the crater-pocked surface of the moon is

anything but smooth. Of course, this is not surprising to you, because you have seen pictures of the moon's surface, some of them taken by astronauts who walked on lunar soil. But try to think of it as Galileo might have when, as the first human to see a magnified moon, he looked upon a surface that for centuries had been regarded as a perfectly smooth sphere. Wouldn't you be surprised and excited by your discovery?

With a telescope or a pair of binoculars that are *firmly mounted* or held against a fixed object, you can observe the moons of Jupiter. Look at them as frequently as possible to see how they change position. It was their movement relative to Jupiter that convinced Galileo that they must be in orbit about the sun's largest planet.

With the same optical device, you can see, as did Galileo, that the Milky Way is not a fuzzy film but rather a large number of individual stars. Finally, use your telescope or binoculars to look at stars and at whatever planets are visible in the evening or early morning sky. What do you notice about a star as compared with a planet? You will probably observe the same difference that Galileo noticed nearly 400 years ago.

GALILEO ON MOTION
Galileo often wrote in dialogue form. One of the characters in his dialogues was Simplicio, who represented the ancient "Ptolemaic" point of view, developed by the second-century astronomer Ptolemy, which placed the earth at the center of the universe, with all bodies revolving around it. Salviati, who had a Copernican viewpoint, might well have been Galileo expressing his own analysis. Unfortunately, someone convinced Pope

Urban VIII that Simplicio was a caricature of the pope himself. Galileo was brought before the Inquisition on charges of heresy and forced to renounce his views.

In the dialogue that follows, we see Salviati maintaining not that two objects of different weight will fall side by side, but that they will fall at very nearly the same rate, whereas Aristotle had argued that the rate of fall was proportional to an object's weight.

> Simplicio: *Your discussion is really admirable; yet I do not find it easy to believe that a bird shot falls as swiftly as a cannonball.*
>
> Salviati: *Why not say a grain of sand as rapidly as a grindstone? . . . Aristotle says that "an iron ball of one hundred pounds falling from a height of one hundred cubits [150 feet] reaches the ground before a one-pound ball has fallen a single cubit." I say they arrive at the same time.*

INVESTIGATION 6:
FALLING OBJECTS
Aristotle held that falling bodies moved toward the center of the earth (the natural position for falling objects, according to him) with a speed that was proportional to their weight. Galileo is reported to have tested Aristotle's theory by dropping two cannonballs, one ten times heavier than the other, from the Leaning Tower of Pisa. It's highly unlikely that he actually did the experiment; but a similar experiment was performed by

the Dutch scientist Simon Stevinus at an earlier date, and Galileo may have been aware of it. In any case, you can test the theory for yourself in a manner similar to the method Stevinus probably used.

Hold a tennis ball and a baseball side by side. Release both objects at the same time. Does the baseball reach the floor well ahead of the tennis ball or do they fall side by side?

For a second experiment, take a piece of paper and release it simultaneously with a heavy book from the same height. Which object reaches the floor first: Can you explain why?

To remove the effect of air resistance on the paper, place it on top of the book, being sure that no part of the paper extends beyond the book's cover. Again, release the book, this time with the paper on the book's top surface. How do the two objects fall this time? What do you conclude?

Finally, take the sheet of paper and squeeze it into as small a sphere as possible. Again, release the paper ball and a baseball side by side. How do they fall under these conditions? Do you see why Galileo had reason to dispute Aristotle's teachings?

INVESTIGATION 7:
THE WAY THINGS FALL

Galileo was not content to show that Aristotle was wrong. Knowing that all objects fall in the same manner if the effects of air resistance are negligible, he sought to understand how, in fact, objects do fall. He realized that the speed of an object increases as it falls, but the rate of fall was so great that he could not measure the time accurately. So he ingeniously devised a means of diluting gravity. Instead of letting a ball fall straight to the floor, Galileo allowed it to roll along an inclined plane. Gravity still acted on the ball, causing it to roll faster and faster as it descended; however, the time required for the ball to reach the end of the incline was now much longer than it would have been if it simply fell straight down.

Salviati describes the method used by Galileo:

> A piece of wooden molding ... about twelve cubits long ... was taken; on its edge was cut a channel a little more than one finger in breadth; having made this groove very straight, smooth, and polished, and having lined it with parchment ... we rolled along it a hard, smooth, and very round bronze ball ... noting ... the time required to make the descent.

Galileo used a water clock, a large elevated vessel of water with a narrow pipe emerging from the bottom, to measure the time. When the ball was released, water was allowed to flow from the vessel through the pipe. When the ball reached the end of the channel, the water flow was stopped. The weight of the water collected was used to measure time.

You can do the same experiment using a long, rigid, very straight piece of aluminum or steel channel and a steel ball that will roll easily along the channel. A water clock like the one shown in figure 6 can be used to measure time. When a partner releases the steel ball by giving the pencil that blocks it a sharp pull forward (not

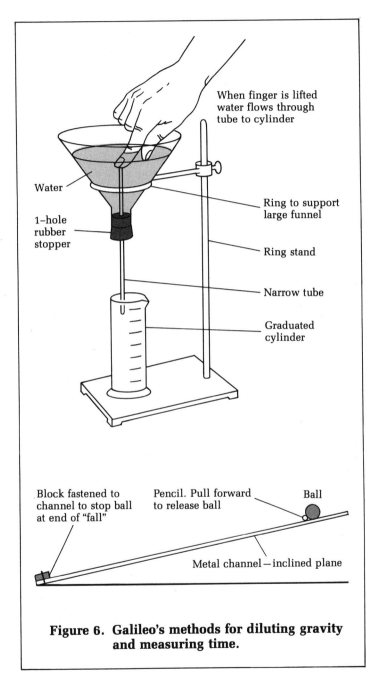

When finger is lifted
water flows through
tube to cylinder

Water

1–hole
rubber
stopper

Ring to support
large funnel

Ring stand

Narrow tube

Graduated
cylinder

Block fastened to
channel to stop ball
at end of "fall"

Pencil. Pull forward
to release ball

Ball

Metal channel—inclined plane

**Figure 6. Galileo's methods for diluting gravity
and measuring time.**

upward, which may give the ball a spin backward), you can remove your finger from the top of the plastic tube that exits the bottom of the large funnel through a rubber stopper. When the ball reaches the wooden bumper at the bottom of the track, place your finger on the tube again. The time can be measured in terms of the weight or volume of water in the collecting vessel because the amount of water that flows from the funnel is proportional to the time it flows.

Make several runs, as Galileo did, for each of a number of different distances. You might let the ball roll 1.0 m, 0.75 m, 0.50 m, and 0.25 m. Take the average time for each distance, being careful to discard data when you are sure the "clock" was started or stopped too soon or too late, or when the ball was not released or did not roll properly.

Using the data you have collected, plot a graph of the distance the ball rolled as a function of the time *squared*. What do you find?

Salviati reported Galileo's results:

> . . . in such experiments, repeated a full hundred times, we always found that the spaces traversed were to each other as the squares of the times. . . .

Do your results agree with Galileo's? That is, do you find your graph to be a straight line?

Galileo realized that the distance traveled would be proportional to the time squared only if the acceleration (the ratio of the change in velocity to the change in time) were constant. To see why this is true, look at the graph in figure 7.

The diagram is an approximate velocity-time

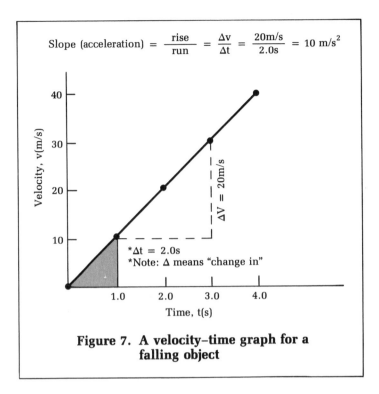

Figure 7. A velocity–time graph for a falling object

plotting for a falling object. We see that after one second the object has a velocity of 10 m/s (meters per second), after two seconds it is 20 m/s, after three seconds it is 30 m/s, and so on. Now the area under this graph at any point in time gives the distance the object has traveled. After all, distance equals velocity multiplied by time, whether the velocity is constant or changing. After one second the distance traveled (the area under the graph) is the area of the little triangle with a base of one second and an altitude of 10 m/s, which represents a distance of 5 meters. After two seconds the total area under the graph is 20 m; after three seconds it is 45 m, etc. The following table shows the total distance fallen after each of the first four seconds.

Time (s)	Distance fallen (m)
1	5
2	20
3	45
4	80

As you can see, when the time doubles, the distance fallen increases four times. Reasoning in reverse, we can see, as Galileo did, that if the distance traveled is proportional to the time squared, the acceleration must be constant.

Galileo had no means of measuring the short time intervals required to estimate the actual acceleration of falling bodies, but by diluting gravity he was able to show that falling objects do indeed accelerate at a fixed rate.

To see or hear this in another way, **have an adult with carpentry skills help you build** blocks on a clothesline, as shown in figure 8. A hole is drilled in the center of each block so that the line can pass through it. Then with knots or tape the blocks are set at distance intervals of one, four, nine, and sixteen units (the squares of 1, 2, 3, and 4) from the line's end. For example, the blocks might be 6 inches, 2 feet, 4.5 feet, and 8 feet from the floor when the line is held vertically **by an adult standing carefully on a stepladder**.

When the blocks are allowed to fall, you will hear each of them strike the floor with a "click." If the blocks fall with constant speed, what will you hear? If they fall with constant acceleration, then

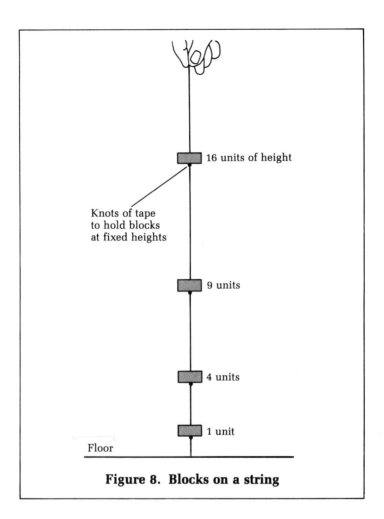

Figure 8. Blocks on a string

the distance they fall is proportional to the time squared. So, in two units of time a block will fall four times as far as it will in one unit of time. In three units of time it will fall nine times as far as in one unit of time, etc.

What do you hear when the blocks are allowed to fall? Are the intervals between clicks

[41]

spaced in the same way as the distances (1, 4, 9, 16)? Or are the clicks equally spaced in time? What do you conclude about the falling blocks? Do they fall as Galileo would have predicted?

INVESTIGATION 8:
PROJECTILES
Galileo was the first person to correctly explain and predict the path of a projectile, although Leonardo da Vinci had described the path a century earlier in an unpublished notebook.

Galileo assumed the vertical and horizontal motions of a body to be independent of one another. In other words, an object will be subject to the same vertical acceleration whether it is moving horizontally or not. A body launched with a certain horizontal velocity will continue to move with the same horizontal velocity because there is nothing to change its horizontal motion (assuming air resistance is negligible).

To test this idea, you can predict the path of a projectile, map it, then check to see if the projectile follows the path you predicted. Begin by building a ramp like the one shown in figure 9.

Clamp the ramp to a level surface, such as a low table or a heavy box. Release a small steel ball or a marble from the top of the ramp a dozen or so times. Let the ball land on a piece of carbon paper placed over the paper "runway," carbon-side down. If you release the ball from the same position each time, the ball should land at about the same place on the paper. Draw a circle around the clustered landing points that have been marked on the white paper where the ball hit the carbon paper, and measure the horizontal distance from the bottom of the plumb line to the center of the

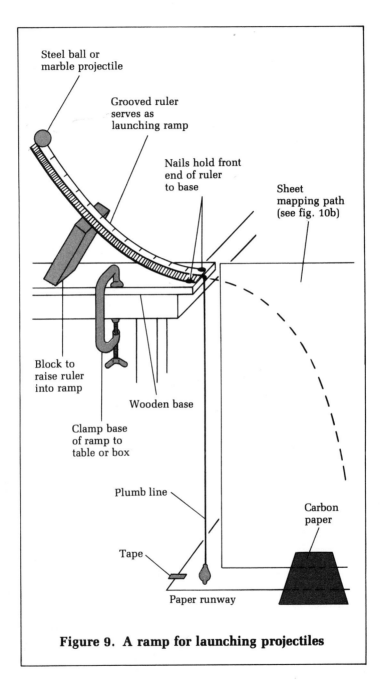

Figure 9. A ramp for launching projectiles

Steel ball or
marble projectile

Grooved ruler
serves as
launching ramp

Nails hold front
end of ruler
to base

Sheet
mapping path
(see fig. 10b)

Block to
raise ruler
into ramp

Wooden base

Clamp base
of ramp to
table or box

Plumb line

Carbon
paper

Tape

Paper runway

[43]

circle. This will give you the average horizontal distance the ball traveled after being launched from the end of the ramp.

The flight time of the projectile can be determined from the graph in figure 10a, which was obtained from the data in figure 7. From the graph we can obtain the equation

$$h = 5 \text{ m/s}^2 \times t^2$$
or
$$h = \tfrac{1}{2} gt^2,$$

where g is the vertical acceleration of falling bodies, which is approximately 10 m/s² (meters per second squared), h is the height of fall, and t is the time of fall. As we found earlier, the height fallen (h) is proportional to the square of the time. The proportionality constant in this case is simply ½ g or half of 10 m/s².

To find the time of flight, you simply take the square root of h divided by ½ g. Suppose the ball's launch position is 0.50 meter higher than the point where it lands. The time of flight then will be

$$t = \sqrt{\frac{0.50 \text{ m}}{5.0 \text{ m/s}^2}} = \sqrt{0.10 \text{ s}^2} = 0.32 \text{ s}$$

Knowing the flight time, you can now find the horizontal velocity, which Galileo predicted would not change throughout the projectile's flight. Suppose the ball traveled 0.32 meter horizontally as it fell through the 0.50 meter height. Since the time it took to travel the 0.32 m was 0.32 second, its horizontal velocity was 0.32 m/0.32 s = 1.0 m/s. With this information, or whatever your data turns out to be, you can now predict the flight path of the projectile using a table like the following. In this table we use the same data mentioned above—a flight time of 0.32 second and a horizontal velocity of 1.0 m/s. The height fallen is measured from the bottom of the ball at the end of the "launching pad."

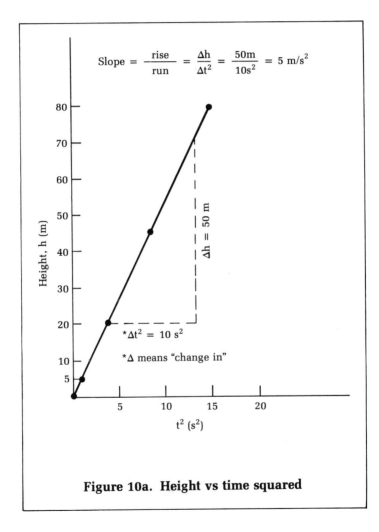

Figure 10a. Height vs time squared

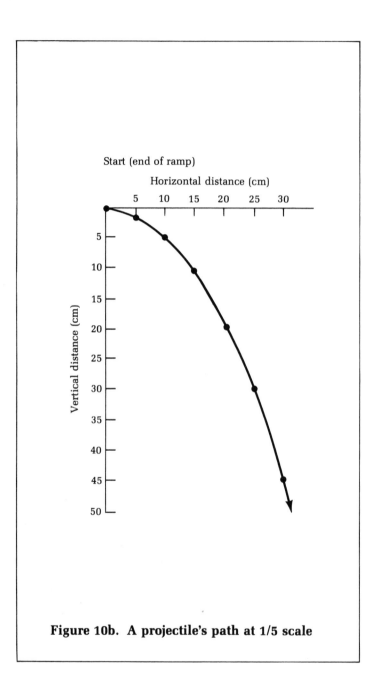

Figure 10b. A projectile's path at 1/5 scale

Time (s)	Height fallen (cm) $(h = \frac{1}{2} gt^2)$	Horizontal distance traveled (cm) (distance = velocity $\times$ time)
0.05	1	5
0.10	5	10
0.15	11	15
0.20	20	20
0.25	31	25
0.30	45	30

Using the data in the table will give the predicted path (shown at one-fifth scale) in figure 10b. If you map the path you have predicted carefully on a large piece of cardboard and place it next to the launch pad as shown in figure 9, you can check to see if the predicted path matches the path actually traveled by the projectile. What do you find? Do the two motions, vertical and horizontal, seem to be independent of one another?

WILLIAM HARVEY (1578–1657)

The advancements in physics and astronomy that were taking place through the efforts of Copernicus, Tycho Brahe, Galileo, Kepler, and others were accompanied by similar developments in biology. Andreas Vesalius (1514–1564) was a great artist and anatomist. His book *De Humani Corporis Fabrica* contains marvelous drawings of his dissections of cadavers. Examine some of Vesalius's drawings, which can be found in many librar-

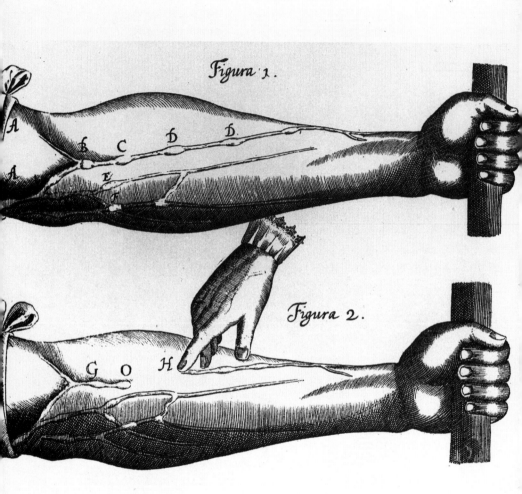

An engraving of William Harvey's experiments on
bandaged arms. By applying pressure to the blood
vessels, Harvey demonstrated the mechanism of blood
circulation in veins and arteries.

ies. It was Vesalius who showed that women and men have the same number of ribs (twelve pairs). People had assumed from the biblical story of Eve's creation from Adam's rib that women had one more rib than men.

William Harvey, who was born fourteen years after Vesalius died, began to experiment with living animals after studying anatomy. His knowledge of anatomy and his experiments led him to conclude that blood did not ebb and flow as the Greek physician Galen had maintained, but rather circulated from the heart through arteries to the body and then back to the heart through veins. Harvey noted that the auricles of the heart were separated from the more muscular ventricles by one-way valves that would allow blood to flow only from auricle to ventricle. At the junction between arteries and ventricles there were again one-way valves that would allow flow from ventricle to artery and not the reverse. Harvey also found valves in the veins that allowed blood flow only toward the heart.

When he tied off an artery in an animal, the artery always bulged on the side toward the heart. When a vein was tied off, the bulge always appeared on the side away from the heart. Just as Galileo, Copernicus, and Kepler had been ridiculed for doubting the wisdom of the ancients, so Harvey was refuted by colleagues who quoted from Galen but never took the time to repeat Harvey's experiments.

INVESTIGATION 9: BLOOD FLOW
Through your science teacher you may be able to buy or obtain a sheep or a beef heart. Another possible source of such hearts would be a butcher

shop or a slaughterhouse. Once you have the heart, **you can dissect it under adult supervision** to see the one-way valves and chambers that Harvey observed. From your observations, how do you think blood moves through the heart?

Even if you can't obtain a heart, you can find evidence for the one-way circulation of blood in your own arm. Find a clearly visible vein on the back of your hand or on the inside of your forearm. If you have trouble seeing a vein, let your arm hang down for a minute or two and open and close your fist so that blood will tend to collect in the veins of your hand and forearm.

Hold one finger firmly near the lower end of a vein so as to seal it off. Use another finger to "sweep" blood in the vein from the point where you have closed it off toward the heart. You will find that you can empty a part of the vein. In fact, with care you can locate some of the valves in your veins. Can you sweep the blood away from the heart? What do your observations tell you about the way blood can flow in your veins? How many valves can you locate? Are they all the same distance apart?

Try the same experiment on the same veins in other people. Are the results the same? Are the valves in their veins located at the same places as the valves in your veins?

FRANCESCO REDI (1626?–1697 or 1698)

Redi, who was a poet as well as a scientist, had read Harvey's work and was particularly interested in Harvey's speculation that small living things such as the maggots that appear on decaying organic matter might arise from seeds or eggs too small to be seen. It had been assumed for ages that these organisms arose by spontaneous generation, that somehow the decaying matter itself spawned the life that fed on it. Redi set out to test this idea.

INVESTIGATION 10:
DOES LIFE ARISE BY
SPONTANEOUS GENERATION?
Redi's investigation should be repeated in the summer when there are flies around. Obtain several glass vessels that can be sealed and will not break when heated. (Canning jars are good.) Under adult supervision, heat the vessels in a pressure cooker or autoclave to sterilize them. In each vessel place a piece of recently cooked meat that has not been in contact with flies. Leave several of the vessels open so flies can enter. Seal several with stoppers, and cover several with gauze so that air can enter the vessel but flies can't. Put the vessels in a place where there are flies and leave them for several weeks. Observe the vessels carefully on a daily basis.

In which vessels do you find maggots? Can you find eggs in or on any of the vessels? In which vessels does the meat eventually rot? What can you conclude from your observations?

Upon completion of the experiment, carefully discard the contents in the garbage or compost pile, then clean the vessels thoroughly with soap and hot water.

4
OTHER GIANTS
OF EARLY SCIENCE

After Galileo and others had established a method of scientific inquiry based on experiment and mathematical analysis, a number of natural philosophers eagerly began to practice the new approach, making startling discoveries of their own. Among them was a young Italian who came to Galileo's side just prior to his death.

EVANGELISTA TORRICELLI
(1608–1647)

After hearing of a book on mechanics by Torricelli, Galileo, who was by then an old man and nearly blind, invited Torricelli to Florence in 1641. Torricelli was delighted to have the opportunity to converse with this man whom he greatly admired. He remained in Florence as Galileo's secretary and companion for the last three months of Galileo's life. While there, Galileo told him a story that led Torricelli to perform the experiment for which he is best remembered.

A craftsman familiar with the operation of lift pumps was called into a mine to try to fix a pump that would no longer lift water from a deep well. After checking the pump, the craftsman reported that the fault lay not with the pump but with the fact that the water was more than 34 feet below the pump. The craftsman told the owner of the mine that a lift pump could not raise water more than 34 feet. Galileo was troubled by this story because the operation of a lift pump was explained by the old Aristotelian concept "Nature abhors a vacuum." As the piston in the pump rose, it created a partial vacuum in the cylinder, causing water to enter the cylinder because "Nature abhors a vacuum" and so will fill any attempt to create one. If this explanation were true, why should nature not abhor a vacuum more than 34 feet above the water?

Although Aristotle had taught that air was weightless, it was becoming fashionable to challenge the master, and Torricelli responded accordingly. If air does have weight, he argued, then it would act like a giant sea and exert a force on everything within it, including the water at the bottom of a mine. When the pressure above the water was lowered by a pump, the water would be forced up the pipe by the air and enter the pump's cylinder. If the weight of the air could only push water to a height of 34 feet, then the pump would be useless when placed more than 34 feet above the water's surface.

To test his hypothesis, Torricelli took a tube about three feet long, sealed it at one end, and laid it in a trough of mercury. When he raised the closed end of the mercury-filled tube, keeping the open end beneath the mercury surface, he found that the tube remained filled with mercury until the mercury level in the tube was 30 inches above the mercury in the trough. Torricelli had invented the barometer. He argued that the empty six-inch-long space at the top of the tube when vertical must be a vacuum because it had been filled, was now empty, and no air bubbles had been seen rising in the tube.

Because mercury is 13.6 times as dense as water, Torricelli reasoned that a column of water could be supported by the air's weight to a height 13.6 times as high as the mercury column. Thirty inches is, of course, 2.5 feet, and 13.6 multiplied by 2.5 feet is just 34 feet. Torricelli's hypothesis explained the pump's failure very nicely.

It would be fun to repeat Torricelli's experiment, but it's not recommended because mercury is poisonous. However, you could do the experiment using water instead of mercury if you can find **an adult to help you** and a stairwell more than 34 feet high.

INVESTIGATION 11:
A WATER BAROMETER
You'll need some thick-walled clear plastic tubing that is about 35 feet long. Slowly add this tubing to a large container (a washtub is good) partially filled with *warm* water (to reduce the formation of air bubbles) dyed with food coloring to improve visibility. The tub should be at the bottom of the tall stairwell. Allow water to enter the tubing as you slowly submerge and coil it in the tub of water. There should be no air bubbles in the tube. Once all the tubing is filled, place a small cork or rubber stopper into the top end of the tube under water. Have an adult carry the sealed end of the

long tube slowly up the staircase while you hold the lower end beneath the water. How high up is the column of water before it finally leaves a space at the top of the tube? Why do you think Torricelli chose to use mercury?

BLAISE PASCAL (1623–1662)

Another test of Torricelli's hypothesis was suggested by Blaise Pascal. His experiment, which is easily done today, was carried out in 1648.

Torricelli's explanation of the lift pump failure and of his new instrument, the barometer, came to be known as the sea of air hypothesis because it assumed that the air, like water in the sea, exerts a pressure. Since pressure increases as we go deeper into the sea (or any water, for that matter), it follows that since we live at the bottom of the sea of air, air pressure should increase as we descend in the atmosphere.

To test the sea of air hypothesis and Aristotle's idea that nature abhors a vacuum, the French mathematician and physicist Blaise Pascal designed a simple, but ingenious, experiment.

INVESTIGATION 12:
TESTING THE SEA OF
AIR HYPOTHESIS
On September 19, 1648, Pascal's brother-in-law, Périer, carried out the experiment Pascal proposed but could not perform himself because of poor health. You can do the same experiment in a somewhat easier manner than Périer, for he had to carry and assemble a mercury barometer several times as he ascended the Puy de Dôme mountain in France. At the same time, a friend at the

base of the mountain checked an identical barometer periodically to be sure the height of the mercury column remained constant.

You can use an aneroid barometer, which is much easier to carry and avoids the need for the toxic element mercury. Read the barometer at the foot of a tall building. Then carry the barometer with you as you ride the elevator to the top of the building. How does the reading on the barometer at the top of the building compare with the reading on the first floor? To be sure the barometer reading has not changed at street level, return to the bottom floor and again read the barometer.

A better experiment would be to actually carry the barometer up a tall mountain in a car or on foot, or, with your parents' permission, to ascend to several thousand feet while holding the barometer in an airplane that is not pressurized.

What happens to the barometer reading as you move upward in the atmosphere? Do your results enable you to decide between the sea of air hypothesis and the idea that nature abhors a vacuum? If so, which hypothesis offers the better explanation of the results you obtained? Can you think of any other explanation for your results?

GIOVANNI DOMENICO CASSINI (1625–1712)

Cassini is often known as Jean Dominique Cassini because he spent half his life in France after leaving Italy to work at the Paris Observatory at the invitation of Louis XIV. By the time he came to France, Cassini had determined the rotational periods of Jupiter and Mars, as well as the orbits of Jupiter's moons. He went on to discover four moons of Saturn and found that the ring around Saturn was actually a double ring with a space between that became known as Cassini's division. But his most important work was determining the distance to Mars, which he did by measuring the parallax of Mars. Cassini in Paris and his colleague, Jean Richer, in French Guiana, about 5,000 miles away, simultaneously viewed Mars against the background of the distant stars. By comparing their results, Cassini calculated that Mars had an orbit with a radius about 80 million kilometers (50 million miles) greater than the earth's. The relative radii of the orbits of the planets had been known since Kepler showed that the quotient of a radius (R) of a planet's orbit cubed to its period (T) squared was the same for all planets. That is,

$$\frac{R^3}{T^2} = K,$$

where K is a constant.

Once the distance between the earth and Mars was established, it was possible to determine the actual radii of the orbits of all the planets.

INVESTIGATION 13:
USING PARALLAX TO
MEASURE DISTANCE
You probably can't arrange to have an astronomer friend observe Mars against the background of the distant stars from a point several thousand miles away, but you can use the method of parallax as Cassini did to measure the distance to an object that is considerably closer than some very distant one.

To understand what is meant by parallax, hold a pencil at arm's length. Look at it first with one eye and then with the other. Notice how the pencil appears to shift with respect to more distant objects. This shift is called parallax. If you hold a second pencil on top of the first one, they will not shift relative to one another. Objects that are the same distance away show no parallax, one to the other. If you move one of the pencils closer to your eye, you'll see that now there is parallax between them when you close first one eye and then the other or if you shift your head from side to side.

To use parallax to measure distance, sight on two objects that form a straight line but are at greatly different distances from you. One object might be a mountain, a monument, or a steeple a mile or so away, the other a star or some other faraway object. The distant object should be so far away that very nearly parallel light rays are coming from it to points a few meters from you. Walk a few steps at right angles to your line of sight and look again. The two objects are no longer along the same line of sight.

To measure the distance to the nearer object, we will use the distant object as a reference point and use the parallax between the two objects to find the desired distance. With a board like the one in figure 11a, use two pins to establish a sight line from your eye through the near and distant objects. Now measure a baseline of several meters or yards perpendicular to your line of sight. Move to the other end of the baseline and again sight along the two pins to the distant reference star, mountain, or whatever. Use a third pin (pin 3) together with pin 2 to mark the new line of sight

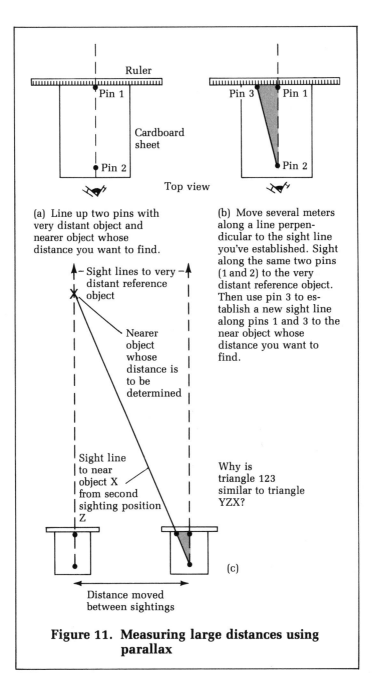

Ruler

Pin 1

Cardboard
sheet

Pin 2

Top view

(a) Line up two pins with
very distant object and
nearer object whose
distance you want to find.

Pin 3   Pin 1

Pin 2

(b) Move several meters
along a line perpen-
dicular to the sight line
you've established. Sight
along the same two pins
(1 and 2) to the very
distant reference object.
Then use pin 3 to es-
tablish a new sight line
along pins 1 and 3 to the
near object whose
distance you want to
find.

Sight lines to very
distant reference
object

Nearer
object
whose
distance is
to be
determined

Sight line
to near
object X
from second
sighting position
Z

Why is
triangle 123
similar to triangle
YZX?

(c)

Distance moved
between sightings

**Figure 11. Measuring large distances using
        parallax**

to the nearer object. Because of parallax the near-er object has now shifted its apparent position relative to the distant reference object. (See figure 11b.)

From the distances between pins 1 and 3, pins 1 and 2, and the length of the baseline, you can determine the distance to the nearer object. Figure 11c will help you to understand this. The dotted sight lines to the distant reference object are parallel because the reference is so far away. What is the distance to the nearer object?

How could you determine the distance to the nearer object if it were not possible to align it with the distant reference object? See if you can do this same experiment using a camera in place of the board and pins. Why did Cassini have to use a baseline of several thousand miles in order to measure the distance to Mars?

ROBERT BOYLE (1627–1691)

Boyle was a brilliant child born into the Irish aris-tocracy. As a teenager he studied the works of Galileo and became dedicated to the study of science.

When he was about thirty, Boyle learned that Otto von Guericke (1602–1686) in Germany had built an air pump that enabled him to evacuate vessels so as to obtain excellent vacuums. In fact, Guericke, who was somewhat of a showman, had demonstrated that teams of horses could not pull apart metal hemispheres that he had put together and then evacuated with his air pump. With the help of Robert Hooke (see page 65), Boyle improved upon Guericke's pump and used the pump to show that in a vacuum Galileo was right—a feather and a piece of lead both fall with the same acceleration.

His work with an air pump led him to investigate air and to discover the law which bears his name. In his original research, Boyle used a J-tube sealed at the top of the short loop. He trapped air in the short, sealed side of the J-tube, then compressed it by adding mercury to the long side. In the experiment that follows, you will not use mercury because it is poisonous, but your results should be similar to those that Boyle obtained.

INVESTIGATION 14:
BOYLE'S LAW
To carry out an investigation similar to Boyle's, you will need a plastic cylinder and syringe (the 35-milliliter size works well), like that shown in figure 12a.

The narrow or nozzle end of the syringe should be tightly sealed with a small cap or in some other way. A thin wire can be used to insert the piston to its initial setting in the cylinder (somewhere between 30 milliliters and 35 milliliters), as shown in figure 12b. The wire will allow air to enter or leave the cylinder so that initially the pressure will be the same on both sides of the piston. After the wire has been removed, give the stage that rests on the piston a little shove to free it from friction. If the piston does not bounce back up, it may need to be lubricated with a small amount of silicone lubricant so that it can slide freely in the cylinder.

Record the initial volume of the air in the cylinder when there is no weight on the platform, then add a brick of a known mass (about 1 kilogram) to the platform. Give the platform another

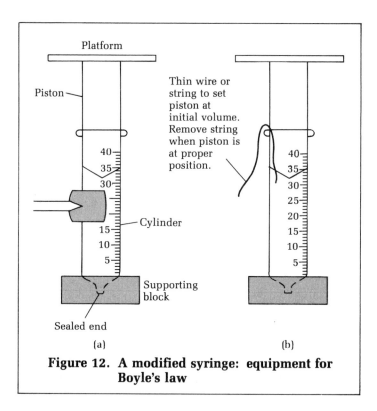

Figure 12. A modified syringe: equipment for Boyle's law

Within the figure:

Platform

Piston

Thin wire or string to set piston at initial volume. Remove string when piston is at proper position.

40
35
30
25
20
15
10
5

Cylinder

40
35
30
25
20
15
10
5

Supporting block

Sealed end

(a)   (b)

short push downward to free it and again record the volume of the gas trapped in the cylinder. Continue to do this until you have added four or five bricks (about 5 kilograms) to the platform. Then remove the bricks one at a time, giving the platform a short push each time, and again record the volume of the trapped air. Take the average of the two volume readings you have made for each number of bricks as the volume for that weight.

Use your data to plot a graph with pressure, in bricks or kilograms, on the horizontal axis and volume on the vertical axis. It's true that bricks aren't units of pressure, but because the cross-sectional area of the piston is constant the load on the piston will be proportional to the pressure.

Based on the graph you have obtained, it should be clear to you that pressure and volume are not proportional. In fact, as the pressure (weight on the piston) increases, the volume decreases. This would suggest plotting pressure as a function, not of volume but of the reciprocal of the volume (1/volume). What do you find when you plot such a graph? What do you conclude?

Now examine the graph a bit more closely. You probably assumed that the pressure was zero when there was no weight on the platform. But as Torricelli taught us, there is a sea of air pushing on the piston. Further, if the pressure were truly zero, there would be nothing to confine the gas and it would expand to an infinite volume. But the value of 1/volume for a volume of infinity would be zero. So it makes sense to extend (extrapolate) your straight line graph of pressure as a function of 1/volume to the point where 1/volume is zero. Since the pressure at this point will be the true zero for pressure, you can change the numbers on the pressure axis to reflect that fact.

From your new graph, what do you conclude about the relationship between pressure and the inverse of volume? Boyle arrived at the same conclusion about 330 years ago.

CHALLENGES
FROM BOYLE
1. Determine the mass of the bricks you used in the experiment, and replot the graph using units of force on the vertical axis instead of bricks. Before you do this you should know that a kilogram weighs 9.8 newtons. To check this for your-

self, hang a kilogram mass on a spring scale calibrated in newtons.

2.   Since pressure is defined as force per unit volume, you will have to know the cross-sectional area of the cylinder in order to determine the pressure in units of newtons per square centimeter or square meter for each reading. How can you find that area?

If you plot pressure, in newtons per square centimeter, as a function of 1/volume, will it change the general shape of your graph? Will it change the shape of the graph if you plot pressure in pounds per square inch as a function of 1/volume?

3.   Use the graphs you have made to determine the pressure exerted by the air. At sea level, air pressure is approximately 10 newtons per square centimeter, which is 100,000 newtons per square meter, or 14.7 pounds per square inch. How closely does your value for air pressure agree with the value given above? If you live at an altitude well above sea level, compare the value from your graph with the reading on a barometer.

4.   From his experiment, Boyle found, as did Torricelli, that the pressure of the air was able to support a column of mercury 76 cm high. Remembering that the density of mercury is about 13.6 grams per cubic cm, show that such a column of mercury is equivalent to a pressure of about 10 newtons per square cm.

5.   In your experiment, the temperature of the enclosed air was probably constant. Do you think Boyle's law would hold if the temperature changed significantly during the experiment?

6. Show that Boyle's law is true not only for air but for other gases as well.

ROBERT HOOKE (1635–1703)

Hooke was a versatile scientist who experimented in various fields. His mechanical skill proved invaluable to Boyle in building an air pump that could create vacuums of better quality than those produced by Guericke. His major discoveries were in biology and physics. Like the great Anton von Leeuwenhoek (1622–1723), he built microscopes and examined microscopic organisms. He was the first to develop a compound microscope, and, while studying the bark of a Mediterranean oak with one of his microscopes, he discovered the structure of cork.

INVESTIGATION 15:
CORK AND CELLS
Have an adult help you cut a very thin slice from a piece of cork. Place the cork on a slide and examine it under a microscope. Notice the pattern of tiny rectangular holes. Hooke referred to these as cells. What do you think was in these cells when the cork was alive?

Hooke went on to show that the cells were filled with a liquid when alive, and the attention of investigators shifted to the contents rather than the rectangular walls.

INVESTIGATION 16:
HOOKE'S LAW
Hooke was also a physicist, and he explained one of his investigations as follows:

Take then a quantity of even-drawn wire, either steel, iron, or brass, and coil it on an even cylinder into a helix of what length or number of turns you please, then turn the ends of the wire into loops, by one of which suspend this coil upon a nail, and the other sustain the weight that you would have to extend it. . . .

Clearly, Hooke's style was not easy to read, but he is describing the making of a spring and the beginning of an experiment that led to a discovery you can share in.

Hang a spring (a screen door spring will do nicely) from a nail or some other firm means of support. Place a meterstick or yardstick behind the spring so you can measure the amount the spring is stretched (S) when various weights (W) are hung on its lower end. If you put the zero point of the meterstick even with the bottom of the spring, the stretch will simply be the new position of the bottom of the spring when a weight is added.

Plot a graph of the weight (W) hung on the spring versus the stretch (S) of the spring. What do you find about the relationship between the force applied to the spring and the amount the spring stretches? This relationship is known as Hooke's law.

CHALLENGES FROM HOOKE
1.   Another discovery made by Robert Hooke has to do with the period of an oscillating spring. Hang a mass of about a kilogram on the lower end of a spring. As it vibrates, determine the period of the spring—the time for the weight to make one

complete oscillation, up and down—as you did for a pendulum bob when it swung back and forth. Now change the amplitude of the oscillation. Does the period change?

2.   How is the period of the oscillating spring related to the weight suspended from it?

3.   Using the graph of stretch versus weight that you made, determine how the work done on a spring is related to its stretch. How is the energy stored in a stretched spring related to its stretch?

5
ISAAC NEWTON

Sir Isaac Newton was a modest man who is reported to have said, "If I have seen further than other men, it is because I stood on the shoulders of giants." The giants on whose shoulders Newton stood were Galileo, Kepler, Brahe, Copernicus, and many of the other early scientists we have already discussed, but Newton was truly the giant of the giants.

SIR ISAAC NEWTON
(1642–1727)

Born on Christmas Day in 1642, Newton is regarded by many as the most brilliant scientist and mathematician who ever lived. His father died before he was born, and when his mother remarried several years later, Isaac was sent to live with his grandparents. Before his late teenage years, he was only an average student who was curious about the world, and enjoyed drawing,

Sir Isaac Newton (1642–1727), perhaps the greatest scientist who ever lived. On his tombstone are these words: "Mortals, congratulate yourselves that so great a man has lived for the honor of the human race."

building models, and constructing mechanical devices such as water clocks and sundials.

He returned to his mother and stepfather in the late 1650s to work on their farm, but he was clearly not cut out to be a farmer, and his uncle and schoolmaster convinced his mother that he should be sent to Cambridge to pursue his studies. He was at Cambridge from 1660 to 1665. While there he met Isaac Barrow, the Lucasian professor of mathematics at the university, who encouraged him to pursue a career in mathematics and natural philosophy. (The word *science* was not used to describe such work until the nineteenth century.)

Newton spent the time from the autumn of 1665 to the spring of 1667 isolated at his mother's farm in the little town of Woolsthorpe. Cambridge University was closed throughout that period because of a plague which took many lives. Those eighteen months were the most productive in Newton's life. As he later said, "For in those days I was in the prime of my age for invention, and minded mathematics and philosophy more than at any time since."

While seated in his mother's yard one day, he saw an apple fall from a tree and at the same time saw the moon in the sky. This observation, we are told, led him to wonder if the same force that pulled the apple to the ground might not also keep the moon in orbit about the earth. Later he wrote:

> I thereby compared the force requisite to keep the moon in her orb with the gravitational force at the surface of the earth and found them to agree pretty nearly.

What he compared was the force acting on the moon at a distance of 60 earth radii from the earth's center with the force acting on the apple at a distance of one earth radius. From Kepler's law $(R^3/T^2 = K)$, and the acceleration of a body moving in a nearly circular orbit $(a = 4\pi^2 R/T^2)$, Newton was led to believe that the gravitational force varied inversely with the square of the distance. He found that the acceleration of the apple was about 3,600 (60^2) times as great as the acceleration of the moon toward the earth. Despite the close agreement between what he predicted from an inverse square law and what he calculated, he put the idea aside for a time. He did this because he probably had to assume that the measurements should be made from the centers of the earth and the moon, which he could not prove at this point, and because his results did not show perfect agreement owing to inaccurate values for the radius of the earth. After he had invented the integral calculus during this same eighteen-month period, he was able to prove that measurements should be made from the center of the earth. Later he assumed that gravitational forces were proportional to the masses of the bodies involved and showed that

$$F = \frac{GM_1 M_2}{r^2}$$

where M_1 and M_2 are the masses of the attracting bodies, r is the distance between them, F is the gravitational force, and G is a universal constant.

What is so striking about Newton is not only the genius revealed by his thinking but the fact that he regarded the force acting on the moon as the same force that acts on bodies near the earth. For centuries thinkers had believed that celestial bodies were not subject to the same laws as earthbound ones. But Newton assumed that the same forces apply to all matter, be it earthly or heavenly. Further, Newton did not attempt to explain why two bodies attract each other. He simply sought the relationship that governs the behavior one can observe.

When asked how he arrived at his ideas, he replied, "I keep the subject constantly before me and wait till the first dawnings open little by little into the full light." It was undoubtedly his ability to concentrate on an idea and to shut out all other stimuli for prolonged periods of time that enabled him to think so deeply and thoroughly. It was this ability to escape to his thoughts that probably explains his absentminded qualities. He would often become so engrossed in an idea that he would forget to eat or sleep.

After the plague years, Newton returned to Cambridge and gave Barrow a copy of the work he had done on what came to be known as calculus. Barrow was so impressed that when he resigned his post, he recommended that Newton succeed him. In 1669, at the age of twenty-six, Newton became the Lucasian professor of mathematics at Cambridge University.

Although his work was brilliant, Newton was not interested in publishing his findings, and when finally persuaded to do so, the criticism of a few skeptics so angered him that he resolved never to publish again. Fortunately, despite harsh criticism from Robert Hooke, who was clearly jealous of Newton, as well as criticism from other less capable people, Newton was convinced by the astronomer Edmund Halley (1656–1742) to publish his findings and thinking about motion. In April of 1686, the first book in a series of three that came to be known as the *Principia* was published, but only because Halley handled all the arrangements and paid for the printing.

Sometime after he had written the *Principia*, Newton was asked how he viewed his contributions to science. Newton replied, "I do not know what I may appear to the world, but to myself I seem to have been only like a boy, playing on the seashore, and diverting myself in now and then finding a smoother pebble or a prettier shell than ordinary, while the great ocean of truth lay all undiscovered before me."

INVESTIGATION 17:
LIGHT THROUGH A PRISM
One of Newton's best-known experiments involves the separation of white light into colors using prisms that he made. Newton was aware of the work of Willebrord Snell (1591–1626) on the refraction of light. He knew that light striking a glass surface at an angle would be bent. To see what he saw when he allowed sunlight to pass through a prism, simply take a prism outside on a sunny day. Move it about in the sunlight. **Don't look directly at the sun.** It can cause permanent damage to your eyes. Turn it until you see a spectrum of color on the ground or on the side of a building. To obtain more impressive results place a piece of white paper where the spectrum is formed. What colors do you see in the spectrum?

For a more controlled experiment, place the

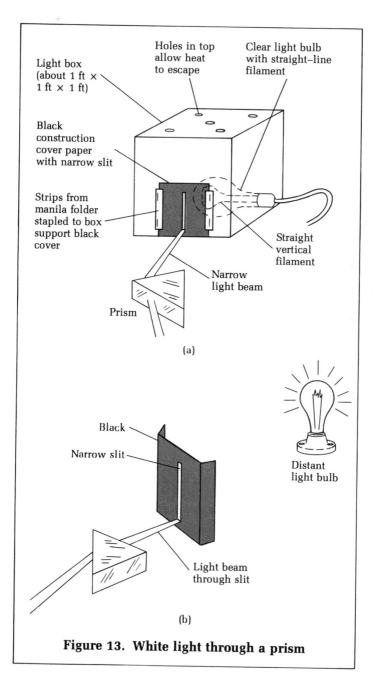

Figure 13. White light through a prism

prism on a narrow beam of white light in an otherwise dark room. You can produce a beam from a light box, as shown in figure 13a, or from a bright light bulb and a piece of black construction paper with a narrow opening in it, as shown in figure 13b.

Newton reasoned that white light, such as sunlight, must consist of a mixture of all the colors in the spectrum. If this were the case, he argued, then a second prism could be used to recombine the colors into white light. You can test this hypothesis for yourself by using a second prism to see if you can bend the colored light in the spectrum together again to reform white light. What do you find? Was Newton right?

Because violet light is bent more than red light, Newton reasoned that the focal length of a lens would be shorter for blue light than for red light. To test this idea, you'll need to make a pair of light "rays" from a source of white light, as shown in figure 14. A jar of water serving as a two-dimensional lens can be placed on two rays coming from a light box. Look carefully at the point on the white paper where the rays are brought together by the refracting effect of the water. Is the focal length of red light greater than the focal length of blue light?

It was evidence from experiments such as the one you have just done that led Newton to build a reflecting telescope. He realized that images formed by magnifying lenses would have a halo of color around them (a problem referred to as *chromatic aberration*). A century later, this problem was largely surmounted by using complex lenses of different materials whose chromatic aberrations canceled each other.

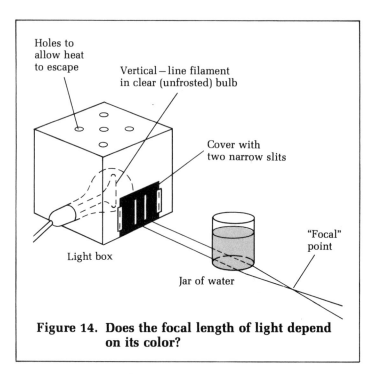

Holes to
allow heat
to escape

Vertical — line filament
in clear (unfrosted) bulb

Cover with
two narrow slits

"Focal"
point

Light box

Jar of water

**Figure 14. Does the focal length of light depend
on its color?**

INVESTIGATION 18:
THE LAWS OF MOTION

Newton's work in optics was original and superb, but it was his ability to develop a magnificent universal model of the universe that best illustrates his genius. His model was based on his three laws of motion, which are stated below in his own words.

Law I:

Every body continues in its state of rest, or of uniform motion in a right (straight) line, unless it is compelled to change that state by forces impressed upon it.

This law, which he credited to Galileo, is commonly called the law of inertia. It simply means that a body maintains its velocity unless a force (a push or pull) acts on it. If it is stationary, it remains stationary. If it is in motion, it maintains its motion. It was Galileo who first realized this fundamental law. Most people, including Aristotle, thought that bodies naturally came to rest. But Galileo and Newton realized that the only reason most moving bodies stop is because the force of friction causes them to slow down and eventually stop.

Here are some things you can try that confirm the first law of motion.

(a) Build a very long pendulum, as Galileo did, and watch it swing. Why does the pendulum stop and reverse its direction of motion? If you lengthened the pendulum, what would happen to the motion?

(b) Build a long pendulum, pull the bob to one side, and measure its height above the floor. Release the bob and catch it on the opposite side when it reaches its maximum height. How does its height on that side compare with its original height? What does this tell you? If there were no friction at the point of suspension or between the bob and the air, for how long would the pendulum swing?

(c) Push the puck of an air hockey game along the air table. If you have access to an air track in your school, give one of the cars a gentle push along the track while the air pump is on. What do you notice about the motion? If you have a dry ice puck or can make a frictionless air car, give it a push along a smooth, level surface, such as a formica tabletop. Then push the same puck or air car along the same surface when there is no gas emerging from the bottom of the puck or car. What do you notice? What would be true of the motion of any of these objects if you could entirely eliminate friction?

Law II:

The change of motion is proportional to the motive force impressed; and is made in the direction of the right line in which that force is impressed.

By *change of motion* Newton means the time rate of change in momentum (mass × velocity); hence, since the mass of a body doesn't change, the law states that

$$F = \frac{m\Delta v}{\Delta t},$$

where F = force, m = mass, v = velocity, and t = time.

We may define acceleration as

$$a = \frac{\Delta v}{\Delta t}$$

and write Newton's law as $F = ma$.

Consequently, Newton's second law of motion states that the force applied to a body is proportional to the acceleration that the body acquires. Further, the direction of the acceleration will be in the direction of the force.

It was Newton who first made the distinction between weight and mass. He recognized that the ratio of force to acceleration measured the inertia or mass of a body. A massive body, such as a car, will have a small acceleration even if you push on it as hard as you can on a level surface. A less massive body, such as a child's wagon, will have a much larger acceleration when you push on it with the same force you applied to the car.

Normally we measure an object's mass by placing it on one side of an equal arm balance. On the other side we place standard masses until the two sides balance. The force that pulls the masses downward is the gravitational attraction between the masses and the earth. When the balance beam is level, the forces on the two sides of the balance are equal.

If we drop any two masses, say a kilogram and a gram, they both accelerate downward at the same rate as Galileo had demonstrated. Newton realized that because any two masses fall with the same acceleration, the force of gravity, or weight, must be proportional to mass. The proportionality constant is called g.

For falling objects, $F = ma$ becomes $W = mg$ because the force is the weight of the mass (W) and the acceleration is g. Near the earth's surface this constant acceleration is 9.8 m/s^2.

Newton realized that on the moon or on another planet a mass would not have the same weight that it has on the earth. A kilogram mass, which weighs 9.8 newtons on the earth, weighs only 1.7 newtons on the moon because the force of gravity on the moon is much less than it is on the earth.

(a) To see how gravitational forces are related to mass, obtain some standard masses such as a kilogram, half a kilogram, 200 grams, and 100 grams as well as a 0-20-newton spring balance.

Hang different masses on the spring balance and record the data. How is the weight of these objects related to their mass?

(b) Attach a long rubber band to the front end of a laboratory cart loaded with bricks wrapped in heavy paper or with standard flat weights. Stretch the rubber band a fixed amount using a meter stick, as shown in figure 15. Have a partner hold the cart so that it can't move until you give the signal to release it. If you keep the rubber band stretched the same length throughout the run, the force on the cart will be constant. Have a third person at the end of the table to stop the cart before it goes over the edge. A wooden bumper clamped to the table's edge will also help to prevent the cart and bricks from plunging to the floor.

A tape attached to a computer timing device or a paper tape timer can be used to provide a record of the cart's motion. From this record, plot a graph of the cart's velocity as a function of time. What do you notice about the slope of the graph? What does this tell you about the cart's acceleration when the force is constant?

(c) Using identical rubber bands you can double, triple, and quadruple the force by stretching two, three, and four rubber bands attached to the same cart by the same amount that you stretched the single one. How is the acceleration of the cart related to the force applied to it? Do your results agree with Newton's second law of motion?

(d) Next, apply a force of one rubber band to the cart, but in each run reduce the mass by removing a brick. After determining the acceleration for each run, plot a graph of the ratio of the inverse of the acceleration $(1/a)$ as a function of

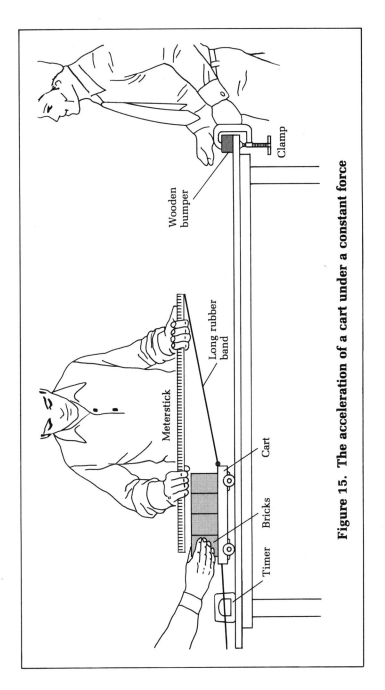

Figure 15. The acceleration of a cart under a constant force

the mass (bricks). What do you conclude from the graph? From your graph, determine the mass of the cart (in bricks).

Law III:

To every action there is always opposed an equal reaction: or the mutual actions of two bodies upon each other are always equal, and directed to contrary parts.

If A pushes on B, B automatically pushes back in the opposite direction on A. (Note that the two opposing forces act on *different* bodies.) When you stand on the floor, you push downward on the floor with a force equal to your weight; the floor pushes upward on you with an equal force. The upward force on you is just equal to your weight; consequently, the net force on you is zero. Since the force on you is zero, your acceleration is zero.

Suppose you and a friend are skating. If you stand at rest facing each other and your friend gives you a push, you will accelerate in the direction he or she pushes you. Your friend, at the same time, will receive an equal push in the opposite direction and accelerate away from you. Assuming there is no friction, once your friend loses contact with you, your acceleration and your friend's acceleration both become zero. Each of you continues to move in the direction you were pushed with constant velocity. Of course, friction will cause you both to slow down and eventually stop, but on ice the frictional forces are weaker and you may travel for quite some time.

(a) Ask a friend with whom you are ice skating or roller skating to stand facing you while you

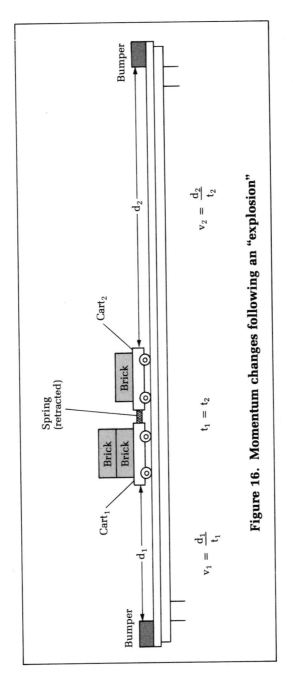

Figure 16. Momentum changes following an "explosion"

are both at rest. Ask him or her to give you a push. What happens? Do your observations agree with Newton's statement of the third law of motion, at least in a qualitative way?

(b) To make the experiment more quantitative, place a lab cart that has a compressible spring within it next to a second cart on a smooth, level table. Place a brick or two on each cart. From the mass of the cart and the bricks on it, record the total mass of each cart. Release the spring by tapping a release mechanism. As the spring "explodes," it pushes the carts apart. To measure the velocity of each cart you can adjust their initial positions before the "explosion" so that the time it takes each of them to get to the bumpers (shown in figure 16) is the same. You can be sure that the times are the same for both carts if you hear a single thud when they collide with the bumpers. If the times are the same, then the velocity of each cart can be expressed simply as the distance it travels before hitting the bumper. Why is the velocity proportional to the distance in this case?

Repeat the experiment a number of times using different masses on the carts. If you're not sure the table is level, turn the carts around and repeat each run. Use the average velocities (distances) of the carts in your calculations.

How do the values for the momentum (mv) of each of the two carts compare in each run? How does the time that cart A pushed on cart B compare with the time that cart B pushed on cart A? From your results, how does the force that cart A exerted on cart B compare with the force that cart B exerted on cart A?

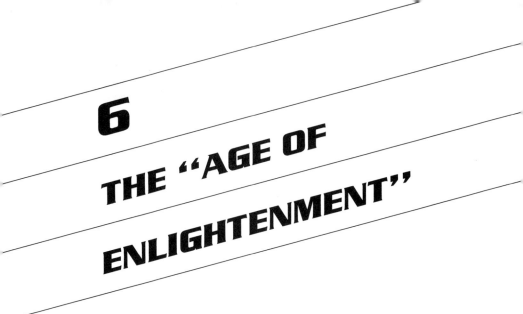

6

THE "AGE OF ENLIGHTENMENT"

The publication of Newton's *Principia* firmly established the power of science and scientific inquiry. Scientists began to probe all aspects of nature and to question the theories and techniques of their contemporaries, as well as those of scientists who had preceded them. Even Newton's theories were subject to the scrutiny of these bold members of a new profession.

JOSEPH BLACK (1728–1799)

Although Joseph Black was a physician, he spent most of his life working as a natural philosopher (a chemist and physicist in today's language). He discovered "fixed air" (carbon dioxide) and recognized that the quantity of heat was not the same as the intensity of heat (temperature). He noticed, too, that ice and snow melt very slowly *without any change in temperature*. When he let snow melt in his hands, he could feel a lot of heat flowing from his flesh even though the temperature of the snow did not change.

In the following investigation you can use Black's method to find how the heat required to melt a fixed mass of ice compares with the heat needed to warm an equal mass of icewater through 8°F (−13°C).

INVESTIGATION 19:
THE HEAT TO MELT ICE

Pour one-third cup of water into a plastic container. Place the container in a freezer and leave it overnight so that the water will freeze thoroughly. Remove the ice from the container and place it in a glass, plastic, or paper cup that you have weighed. Record the time so that you will know how long it takes the ice to completely melt. Weigh the ice and container on a balance. How can you find the mass of the ice alone?

Set the ice aside and fill a measuring cup one-third full with cold water. Add ice cubes to the water, put in a thermometer, and stir until the temperature of the ice and water becomes 32°F (0°C). Can you get the temperature lower than this by adding more ice?

Record the time again and immediately pour the ice cold water into a previously weighed glass or paper cup that rests on a scale. Be sure no ice gets into the cup being weighed. Pour until the mass of the cold water equals the mass of the ice you have set aside to melt. You now have equal masses of melting ice and warming ice water. You can do exactly what Black did: compare the time for the cold water to reach 40°F with the time for the ice to melt *and* warm to 40°F.

Assume, as Black did, that in the same room heat will flow into the ice and cold water at the same rate. How does the heat needed to melt ice compare with the heat needed to warm an equal mass of water through eight degrees?

If the amount of heat needed to warm the ice water from 32°F to 40°F (0°C to 4°C) is called one unit of heat, how many units of heat are required to melt the ice? (Don't forget to subtract the unit required to warm the melted ice from 32°F to 40°F [0°C to 4°C]).

Black found that it took about twenty times as much heat to melt a certain mass of ice as it did to warm the same mass of water eight degrees. How do your results compare with his?

Black did not attempt to explain heat. Like Newton, he realized that scientists could not answer *why* questions. By carrying out experiments, he felt that he and others could come to a better understanding of how heat behaved and only then develop a theory to explain that behavior. Other scientists, contemporaries of Black, believed that heat was an invisible fluid that they called *caloric*. According to this theory, caloric flowed from warm bodies, which possessed a lot of caloric, to cooler bodies, which possessed less of the invisible fluid.

The heat required to melt ice came to be known as the *latent heat of melting*. It was called latent since it did not manifest itself as heat normally does by causing a change in temperature.

Black knew that when water melted or froze, its temperature remained constant. He knew too that the temperature did not change when water boiled or condensed from steam. To measure the latent heat of boiling, he carried out an experiment that was very similar to the one he used to find the latent heat of melting.

INVESTIGATION 20:
THE LATENT HEAT OF BOILING
Pour a pint of water into a saucepan. Measure the temperature of the water, then remove the thermometer. **Because you'll be using high temperatures, ask an adult to help you with the rest of the experiment.** Place the saucepan on a stove, turn on the heat, and record the time. How much time passes before the water is boiling?

Continue heating the water until the moment that it has all boiled away. At that moment, using a pot holder to avoid being burned, remove the empty pan from the stove, and record the time again. How long did it take the water to boil away once it reached the boiling temperature?

Assuming that heat flows into the pan at the same rate throughout the experiment, how does the heat required to raise the water from room temperature to boiling temperature compare with the heat needed to change the water from liquid to gas (to boil away)?

INVESTIGATION 21:
MIXING HOT AND COLD
(a) Before Black began his work, a number of scientists had mixed equal and unequal masses of hot and cold water and found a rule that enabled them to predict the final temperature of the mixture. Using water as cold as 32°F (0°C) and as warm as 120°F (50°C), mix various volumes of hot and cold water. (It's best to use insulated cups in doing these experiments so that the water warms

or cools as slowly as possible before mixing.) See if you can establish a rule that enables you to predict the final temperature. Then test your rule to be sure it works. Why is it reasonable to use volume to measure the amount of water here rather than mass?

(b) It was Black who showed that the rule used to predict the final temperature of a mixture of hot and cold water could not be used to predict the final temperature when two different liquids, or a solid and a liquid, at different temperatures were mixed.

To see what Black found, put some antifreeze (ethylene glycol) and/or cooking oil in a cold place where the temperature is close to 32°F (0°C). When the liquid is cold, mix *equal masses* of hot water and the cold liquid in an insulated cup. You'll see that the temperature of the mixture is not midway between that of the hot water and the cold cooking oil or antifreeze. Be sure to dispose of chemicals properly; do not pour them down the drain.

See if you can establish a rule for predicting the final temperature when equal masses of water and one of these liquids are mixed. If you succeed, see if you can find a rule that works when unequal masses are used.

If you have trouble developing a rule to predict the final temperature when different liquids are mixed, read about specific heat in a textbook or encyclopedia. Then return to your results and see if you can develop a rule that works.

CHALLENGES FROM BLACK
1.   In Investigation 19, why did Black measure the time for the water temperature to rise from

32°F to 40°F (0°C to 4°C) rather than to room temperature? Before you answer this question, you might like to compare the time it takes the temperature of water to rise from 32°F to 40°F (0°C to 4°C) with the time it takes to rise from 42°F to 50°F (5.5°C to 10°C), or from 52°F to 60°F (11°C to 15.5°C). Does heat seem to flow faster from warm air to cold water or from warm air to lukewarm water?

2. If you had done Investigation 19 using equal volumes of water and ice rather than equal masses, would the results have been the same?

3. Place a thermometer bulb in the center of a small container of water. Freeze the water with the thermometer in it. When the water is thoroughly frozen, remove it from the freezer and begin recording the temperature of the ice every five minutes until the water reaches room temperature. Then, using the data, plot a graph of temperature as a function of time. How do you explain the plateau in the graph? Does the rate of heat flow into the ice and water depend on the temperature of the ice or water? How can you tell?

How long does it take the ice to reach a temperature of 32°F (0°C)? To reach a temperature of 40°F (4°C)? From the times plotted on your graph, determine how the heat required to melt ice compares with the heat required to warm the melted ice to 40°F (4°C). Do your results here agree with the results you found when you used Black's method?

How does the heat required to raise the ice from the temperature of the freezer to the melting temperature compare with the heat needed to melt the ice completely? With the heat needed to warm the melted ice to 40°F (4°C)?

BENJAMIN THOMPSON (COUNT RUMFORD) (1753–1814)

Benjamin Thompson was born in Woburn, Massachusetts. During the American Revolution, Thompson sided with the King and escaped to England, realizing he would be permanently exiled should the colonials win the war. After the war he left England for Bavaria, where he served the Elector so well as an administrator that he was made a Count of the Holy Roman Empire. He chose for his title the name Rumford, which was the original name of Concord, New Hampshire, where he had married his first wife, Mrs. Rolfe, a wealthy widow.

Although he was in many ways a rogue, Rumford was a very capable scientist as well as administrator. Many of his experiments were designed to disprove the caloric theory, which he came to doubt because of his work in boring cannons. He found that the brass chips produced when the cannons were bored had the same specific heat as the original brass from which they came. Yet the caloric model of heat predicted the specific heat of the chips should be less because heat had been emitted by the metal during the boring.

You have seen, as did Joseph Black, that large amounts of heat are absorbed when ice melts. Similarly, heat is released when water freezes. Rumford reasoned that if caloric is an invisible fluid, then its loss from water during the freezing process should make the ice less massive than the

[91]

Benjamin Thompson (Count Rumford, 1753–1814).
His experiments led him to reject the view,
widespread at the time, that heat was a substance.

water from which it came. Most scientists agreed with him, but they said the change in mass was small because the density of caloric was small.

Using a very sensitive balance, Rumford found in his first experiment that the frozen water had *gained* mass. He thought that moisture might have condensed on the cold flask or that air currents might have tilted the balance arm slightly. Being of a determined nature, he wrote: "I determined now to repeat the experiment with such variations as should put the matter in question out of all doubt."

Rumford knew that the specific heat of water was greater than that of alcohol and thirty times greater than the specific heat of mercury. If these three substances were allowed to cool through the same temperature range, the water would lose considerably more caloric than alcohol or mercury. Further, since a gram of water loses eighty times as much heat when it freezes as it does when it cools one degree, the heat lost by the water would be dramatically greater than the heat lost by the other two substances if the water was allowed to freeze.

With these facts in mind, Rumford poured equal masses of water, alcohol, and mercury into three identical flasks. The flasks were left in a warm room until all were at the same temperature. After wiping the flasks to remove any dust or moisture, they were sealed and weighed. Small lengths of wire were added to the lighter flasks until all had exactly the same mass.

The flasks containing alcohol and water were placed on opposite sides of a balance and left in a cold room where the water would freeze. When he returned two days later, the water was frozen.

Do you think the beam was still level? Rumford removed the alcohol-filled flask and replaced it with the flask containing mercury. What do you think he found?

INVESTIGATION 22:
LOOKING FOR CALORIC
You can repeat Rumford's experiment quite easily using a plastic container that you can seal, a freezer, a good balance, and some standard masses. Pour some water into the container and seal it. Wipe any dust or moisture from the container and weigh it carefully. (The standard masses have a specific heat considerably less than that of water, so there is no need to use alcohol and mercury.) Leave the masses on the balance, place the container in a freezer, and allow the water to freeze overnight.

The next day you can remove the container from the freezer and place it back on the balance. Has its mass changed? (If the room is humid, moisture may condense on the flask and you will have to wipe the container dry.)

Based on the data you have collected, what do you think Rumford concluded about caloric? Do you think other scientists agreed with his findings? If not, how could they explain his data?

ANTOINE LAVOISIER (1743–1794)

Lavoisier was to chemistry what Newton had been to physics, for it was Lavoisier who demonstrated the falsity of certain widely accepted notions and replaced them with new and unifying ideas about chemistry. He made measurement the touchstone for chemistry as Galileo had for physics. He also developed a sensible language and system for naming elements and compounds. However, he clung to the caloric theory and did not develop a unifying theory to explain the numerical relationships that he and others discovered. This would not happen until John Dalton (1766–1844) first developed an atomic model of matter early in the nineteenth century.

Throughout much of his career Lavoisier was blessed with a wife who was a tremendous help to him. Madame Lavoisier illustrated many of his books, translated books and letters, helped him with experiments, and recorded prodigious notes. She was one of the few women who were actively involved in science prior to the twentieth century.

Lavoisier, who had been a tax collector as well as a scientist, did not survive the French Revolution. He was a victim of the Terror of 1794. When he pleaded that he was a scientist and not a tax collector, the radical, antimonarchist judge replied, "The Republic has no need of scientists." On May 8, 1794, Lavoisier and his father-in-law (also a tax collector) were beheaded. The words of Joseph Louis Lagrange, the French-Italian astronomer/mathematician and friend of Lavoisier, expressed the sentiment of the scientific community when he said, "It took but a moment to cut off his head; it will take a century to produce another like it."

Rumford's experiment with ice demonstrated that there is no mass change when ice freezes. Rumford performed his experiment in an effort to disprove the caloric theory, but earlier, Lavoisier, by careful measurements of mass, had provided evidence for the law of conservation of mass.

INVESTIGATION 23:
LOOKING FOR MASS CHANGES
Lavoisier looked for mass changes, or the lack of mass changes, in chemical and physical changes. You can do the same. In fact, in the last investigation you looked for mass changes when ice froze. Design another experiment to see if there is any change in mass when salt and water are mixed to make a solution.

In both of these experiments, there is no chemical reaction; that is, no new substance is formed. In the following experiment, there will be a dramatic change. **Because the reaction involves chemicals that are poisonous if ingested, you should seek the help of a knowledgeable adult before doing this experiment.**

Prepare a clear solution by adding 15 grams of lead nitrate to 100 milliliters of distilled water. Prepare a second clear solution by adding 7 grams of sodium iodide to 100 milliliters of distilled water. Fill a plastic vial about one-third of the way with one of the solutions. Do the same thing with the other solution in a different vial. Place caps on both vials to avoid evaporation or spilling and weigh them together on a balance. Carefully remove the covers from the vials and pour one solution into the other. Be careful not to lose any liquid. What evidence is there that a chemical change has taken place? Has the chemical change been accompanied by a change in mass?

In 1768 Lavoisier performed a somewhat more complicated experiment to show that water could not be transmuted to earth as many believed. Those who held this belief had evidence to support their position; they did not rely solely on Aristotelian doctrine as they might have a century or two earlier. They could demonstrate that water, when boiled for a long time, gave rise to a sediment.

Lavoisier showed, first of all, that there was no change in the mass of the system (water and sealed glass condenser and boiler) where the boiling took place constantly for a period of more than three months. He then separated the sediment that had formed from the water and showed that the mass of the water had not changed. He reasoned that the sediment must have come from the glass. When he reweighed the glass, its loss in mass was just equal to the mass of the sediment.

One of Lavoisier's major accomplishments was to dispel the phlogiston theory of combustion, which held that flammable materials such as wood contained an invisible fluid called *phlogiston*. When such objects burned, according to the theory, phlogiston was released. After the combustion, the new substance, ash, for instance, was deficient in phlogiston and, therefore, would not burn. This theory, which had been developed by the German chemist Georg Stahl (1660–1734) prior to Lavoisier's birth, was widely accepted by eighteenth-century scientists.

The theory held that it was phlogiston, not air, that was involved in burning. Air served only as a means of transferring phlogiston. For example, charcoal, a substance rich in phlogiston, could be burned and transfer its phlogiston through air to an iron ore. As it gained phlogiston, the ore became iron metal. Stahl believed that metals, such as iron, contained a lot of phlogiston. When they rusted, which Stahl correctly believed to be a slow form of burning, they lost their phlogiston and became calx, a substance that we now know is the oxide of the metal. Stahl was not concerned by the fact that when charcoal turned to ash there was a large loss in mass, while the calx that formed when metal was heated or rusted had *more* mass than the metal. He was not concerned because quantitative studies were not considered important by these early chemists.

By Lavoisier's time, chemists *were* concerned with this difficulty, but rather than discarding the theory, they invented the idea of negative mass. When a metal was heated, they argued, phlogiston left the metal, forming a calx. Because phlogiston had a negative mass, the calx was heavier than the metal. When phlogiston was added to an ore to make a metal, the metal weighed less than the ore because the phlogiston acquired brought with it a negative mass or levity, as some called it. To Lavoisier such an explanation was levity of a different kind.

What Lavoisier did was to provide an alternative theory that made more sense. When it became apparent that he could explain burning, rusting, and the changes that occur when certain metals are heated as a reaction with the oxygen in the air, people began to accept his ideas. This is very common in the history of science. Scientists are reluctant to give up a theory that can explain so much until someone provides a better theory, a theory that explains all that the older one did, but in a more elegant way.

Lavosier showed diamond would not burn in the absence of air, regardless of how much heat (phlogiston) was supplied. In air, in a closed container, the diamond would burn and produce carbon dioxide. When he heated metals such as tin and lead in sealed containers with air, a layer of calx formed on the surface of the metals. Now it was known that the calx weighed more than the metal, yet the total mass of the container and its contents did not change; therefore, the mass added to the calx must have come from the air. Furthermore, if the metal had combined with something in the air to form the calx, then there should be a partial vacuum in the container. When the vessel was opened, air could be heard rushing in to fill the partial vacuum and increasing the total mass of the container.

When Joseph Priestley (1733–1804) visited Lavoisier, he told him of a gas he had prepared by heating the calx (oxide) of mercury. Priestley called the gas "dephlogisticated air," because wood and metals burned in the gas much faster than in air. Priestley believed the rapid burning was produced because the gas had virtually no phlogiston and therefore accepted it readily from substances rich in phlogiston. Lavoisier realized that Priestley had isolated the portion of air that accounts for combustion, a gas that he later called oxygen. He went on to show that air is a mixture that contains primarily oxygen and "azote" (nitrogen).

So keen was his insight that he recognized the process of oxidation could explain an animal's respiration and the source of its energy. The oxygen in air is taken into the blood in the lungs. In the body the oxygen combines with the chemicals in the food we eat to form carbon dioxide and water, both of which we excrete. He saw that this internal and slow process of oxidation was similar to the more rapid form that takes place when

Antoine Lavoisier (1743–1794) conducting
an experiment on human respiration
while his wife takes notes.

something burns. In both cases oxygen combines with oxidizable chemicals to form carbon dioxide and water.

INVESTIGATION 24:
ANIMALS IN "PHLOGISTICATED" AIR
Here's an experiment similar to one that Lavoisier did. Place an animal, such as a mouse, or a number of insects in a closed container that has within it a small birthday candle mounted in a small glob of clay. If the container is open on one end, a little Vaseline or stopcock lubricant along the bottom will help to seal it to a kitchen countertop or table and make it airtight. Use a large magnifying glass to focus bright sunlight on the candle's wick. (Be sure you don't focus the light on the animal(s).) A small lens probably won't work because it can't gather enough light. You may also want to use a small piece of paper fixed near the wick because the paper will ignite easier than the wick. **Ask an adult to work with you since you'll be working with a flame.** In a few minutes the candle will burn out, but as Lavoisier found, the animals will be alive. Do you think the candle used up all the available oxygen when it burned?

INVESTIGATION 25:
CANDLES AND STEEL WOOL
BURNING IN AIR
This experiment is similar to ones that Lavoisier did as he explored ways to separate the components of air.

With an adult to help you, place a birthday candle in a shallow dish of water. A piece of clay can be used to support the candle. Light the candle and let it burn for a minute or two. Then place a tall, narrow jar, such as the kind in which olives are sold, over the burning candle. The candle will soon go out and water will rise in the jar. Some will claim that the water is replacing the oxygen, which has been "all used up" by the burning candle, but if you have done Investigation 24 you will know better. In fact, if you place a little soapy water in the dish and repeat the experiment you'll see why the water rises as high as it does. What do the bubbles tell you about the effect of the heat transferred from the flame to the air?

Now do the experiment in Lavoisier fashion to find the fraction of the air that is "active" (oxygen). Soak a small, loosely made ball of steel wool overnight in a solution that is one part vinegar to two parts water. This will remove the protective oil coating on the steel. Shake off the excess liquid and push the ball of steel wool to the bottom of the tall, narrow jar you used before. Invert the jar and place it in a shallow dish of water dyed with food coloring to improve visibility. Leave the system for a day or two, but observe carefully what happens to the steel wool at the top of the jar and periodically mark the water level in the jar. When no further changes take place, see if you can figure out how Lavoisier determined the fraction of the air that is "active." (He found the active fraction to be about one-fifth of the air. What did you find?)

Lavoisier was careful to keep the temperature constant throughout this experiment. To see why, place the jar and dish in a refrigerator. After several hours measure the level of the water in the jar again. Can you explain why the liquid level has risen? What will happen if you set up the system in a warm place?

JACQUES ALEXANDRE CÉSAR CHARLES (1746–1823)

Charles is best remembered for the law that bears his name; however, he was also the first to recognize that the very low density of hydrogen would make it a more efficient balloon than the hot air balloons being used at the time.

INVESTIGATION 26:
CHARLES'S LAW
Boyle's law expresses the relationship between the pressure and volume of any gas when the temperature is constant. What Charles did was to establish the relationship between the volume and temperature of a gas when the pressure is constant. You can do the same, but **since you'll be using a hot plate or a flame, be sure you are working under the supervision of a knowledgeable adult.**

Use the same syringe that you used in Investigation 14. Be sure that the piston will slide easily in the cylinder. If necessary, add a small amount of lubricant to the piston rings so the piston slides more easily. Use the fine wire to set the piston at about the midpoint of the cylinder. Then place the syringe in a Pyrex container filled with ice and water as shown in figure 11. Stir the ice water mixture thoroughly for several minutes to be sure the gas is at the same temperature as the water. Record the volume at this low temperature, then begin heating the water.

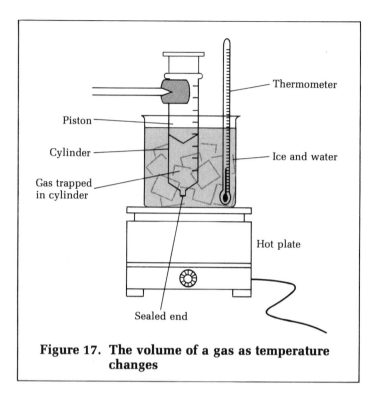

Figure 17. The volume of a gas as temperature changes

Periodically, say at about ten-degree intervals up to 80°C, stop heating the Pyrex container, stir the water thoroughly, and record the volume of air in the cylinder. You may want to tap the piston to be sure it is free to move.

Once you have collected the data, plot a graph of volume as a function of temperature. By what fraction of its original volume does the air expand for each degree increase in temperature? Charles found this fraction to be about 1/273. What do you find? Using your graph or the fraction that you determined, figure out to what temperature the gas would have to be cooled to theoretically reach a volume of zero.

PIERRE LOUIS DULONG (1785–1838), ALEX THÉRÈSE PETIT (1791–1820)

These two scientists worked closely together in determining the specific heats of a large number of elements to see if there was any relationship between this characteristic property and atomic mass.

INVESTIGATION 27:
THE LAW OF DULONG AND PETIT

The specific heat of a substance is the heat per gram that must be transferred to or from the substance to raise or lower its temperature by one degree Celsius. **Since this experiment will require the use of heat, you should work under the supervision of an adult.**

To measure the specific heat of a metallic element such as aluminum, take a piece of the metal (say, about 20 grams), weigh it, suspend it from a string, and place it in a pan of boiling water. (See figure 18.) Since the metal is a good conductor of heat, you can be sure that the metal is at the same temperature as the water (about 100°C) when the water begins to boil again. Transfer the hot metal to 50 grams of cold water in an insulated cup and measure the change in temperature of the water. How can you find the change in temperature of the metal? Why should you transfer the metal to the water as quickly as possible?

To obtain accurate data, the cold water should be several degrees below room temperature before the metal is added and several degrees above room temperature after the hot metal has transferred its heat. Why? If possible, use a thermometer than can be read to ± 0.1°C. If the tem-

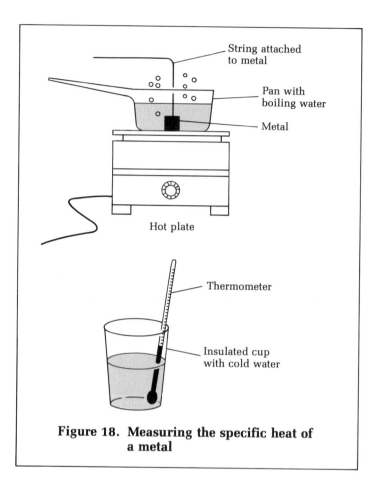

**Figure 18. Measuring the specific heat of
a metal**

perature change of the water is too small, how can
you change the experiment to make it larger?

From the data, you can determine the specific heat of the metal. Suppose that a 20-gram sample of metal is transferred from boiling water to 50
grams (g) of cold water at 17.8°C, and the temperature of the cold water rises to 25.0°C. The heat
transferred to the water, in calories (cal), can easily be determined.

heat transferred to the cold water
$$= 50 \text{ g} \times (25.0°C - 17.8°C) = 360 \text{ cal}$$

This heat must have come from the metal. The metal's temperature changed from 100°C to 25°C. The heat, therefore, that came from 1 gram of the metal to cool it 75°C was:

$$\frac{360 \text{ cal}}{20 \text{ g}} = 18 \text{ cal/g}$$

The specific heat, the heat required to cool 1 gram of the metal 1 degree, was:

$$\frac{18 \text{ cal/g}}{75°C} = 0.24 \text{ cal/g/°C}$$

You may prefer to use the equation that equates the heat transferred to the water (left side of equation) and the heat transferred from the metal (right side of the equation).

$$(\text{mass of water})(\Delta T_{water}) =$$
$$(\text{mass of metal})(\Delta T_{metal})(\text{specific heat}_{metal})$$
$$(50 \text{ g})(7.2°C) = (20 \text{ g})(75°C)(?),$$

where T = temperature.
    We use a question mark (?) for the specific heat because it is unknown.

$$? = \frac{(50 \text{ g} \times 7.2°C)}{(20 \text{ g} \times 75°C)} = 0.24 \text{ cal/g/°C}$$

Try a number of different metals, some with a low atomic weight, such as aluminum, and some with a large atomic weight, such as lead. Copper, tin, zinc, and iron are some other metals that can be easily obtained.

Once you have found the specific heats of a fair number of metals, try what Dulong and Petit did: plot a graph of the reciprocal of the elements' specific heats as a function of their atomic weights. (You can find their atomic weights in a periodic table of the elements.)

What do you conclude? How could you make an estimate of an element's atomic weight if you knew its specific heat?

ROBERT BROWN (1773–1858)

Robert Brown was a botanist who first called the spherical-shaped body found near the center of most living cells the *nucleus*. However, he is best remembered for his discovery of what is now known as *Brownian motion,* a discovery that had far-reaching effects beyond the life sciences.

INVESTIGATION 28:
BROWNIAN MOTION
You can repeat Brown's discovery quite easily. Place some small pollen grains collected from a flower (or some spores from a mushroom moss) in a drop of water on a microscope slide. Add a coverslip and look at the pollen grains or spores through the microscope. Notice how the tiny particles jiggle about. What do you think is causing them to move this way?

Brown thought he was seeing evidence of life within the spores or pollen, but then he examined some dye particles. You can do the same. Put a small amount of india ink or carmine red powder in a drop of water as you did with the pollen and look at the particles under the microscope. What do you see?

You might also capture some smoke under a coverslip using a depression or hanging drop microscope slide. Watch the tiny smoke particles under bright light. Can the motion be explained as a characteristic property of living things? Brown realized his initial explanation was wrong but he could not offer a better one. Can you?

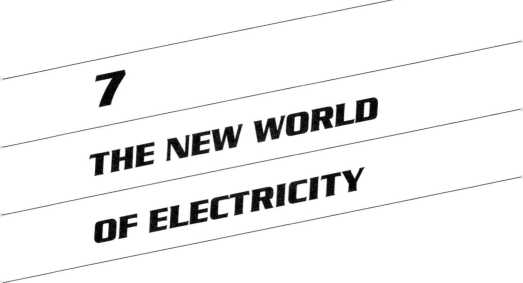

7

THE NEW WORLD

OF ELECTRICITY

Armed with a new physics and a new chemistry, scientists in the early nineteenth century began to ask questions about the nature of matter itself. Their experiments, insights, and theories led to an atomic model of matter and the realization that electrical charges and forces were a fundamental part of atoms, the building blocks of matter. Ultimately, discoveries about electricity led humankind into a very different world.

ALESSANDRO VOLTA (1745–1827)

During the eighteenth century an Italian anatomist, Luigi Galvani (1737–1798), for whom the galvanometer is named, discovered that the legs of frogs he had dissected would twitch during thunderstorms, in the presence of electrical sparks, or, in fact, whenever they made contact with two different metals. Galvani believed that the electricity came from the muscle tissue, and he referred to it as "animal electricity." In 1794 Alessandro Volta, who had experimented extensively with static electricity, wondered if the electrical effects described by Galvani were generated by muscle tissue or by the different metals. To find out, he did an experiment that you can do very easily.

INVESTIGATION 29:
A VOLTAIC CELL
If the source of the electricity that caused the muscles of Galvani's dissected frogs to twitch was to be found in the two different metals and not the muscle tissue, then the metals should be able to produce an electric current in the absence of living tissue. To see if this is possible, clean some pieces of zinc and copper with steel wool or a scouring pad. (You can use aluminum and copper nails, or steel and copper nails if they are more readily accessible.) Prepare a concentrated brine solution by dissolving as much salt (sodium chloride) as possible in some water. Then put the two metals in the brine, as shown in figure 19a. Ordinary drinking glasses or beakers can be used to hold the brine.

Volta actually arranged a large number of these cells in series and detected the flow of electric charge with his fingers. You'll find it easier and less shocking to use a sensitive ammeter.

Based on your results, what do you conclude? Is living tissue required to produce a flow of electric charge?

To reduce the size of his battery, Volta used small discs of different metals with discs of cardboard soaked in brine between the metals, as shown in figure 19b. Such a battery came to be

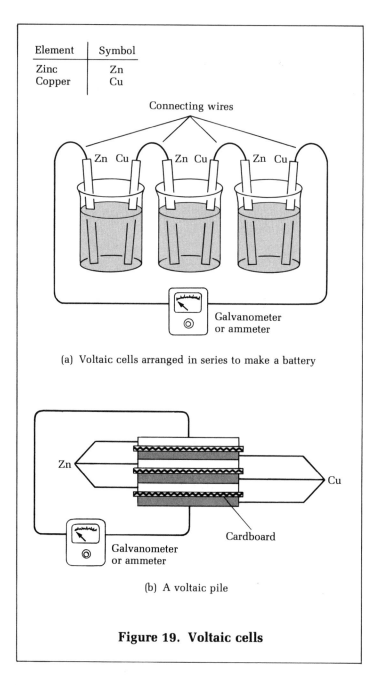

Element	Symbol
Zinc	Zn
Copper	Cu

Connecting wires

Zn Cu   Zn Cu   Zn Cu

Galvanometer
or ammeter

(a) Voltaic cells arranged in series to make a battery

Zn

Cu

Cardboard

Galvanometer
or ammeter

(b) A voltaic pile

Figure 19. Voltaic cells

known as a voltaic pile. You can build a voltaic pile yourself using pieces of copper and zinc separated by pieces of cardboard that have been soaked in brine. They stack up like sandwiches in a lunch box. If you prefer, use pennies and dimes as the metal electrodes. Use two or three discs or coins of each metal to build Volta's modified battery. **Don't use a large number of metal discs; the current produced could be dangerous!** Again, test the battery with an ammeter or galvanometer to see if any charge flows from and to a voltaic pile.

HANS CHRISTIAN OERSTED
(1777–1851)

By 1800, both electricity and magnetism had been studied in great detail by a number of scientists. It was evident that electric charges of the same sign repel one another, while an attracting force is created by charges of opposite sign. Similarly, two north or two south magnetic poles produce a repelling force, but a north magnetic pole is attracted by a south magnetic pole. Despite the similarity in behavior, there are no forces between electric charges and magnetic poles, regardless of sign or polarity.

Because electric charges and magnetic poles seemed to have no effect on one another, scientists had concluded that electricity and magnetism were unrelated. Then, as often happens in science, a surprising discovery led them to change their minds. That discovery was made by Hans Christian Oersted.

Oersted had been appointed professor of physics and chemistry at the University of Copen-

The actual compass used by Oersted in his experiment. To the right is one of the *few* surviving copies of his landmark paper announcing the discovery of electromagnetism.

hagen in 1806. In the winter of 1819–1820, Oersted was preparing a demonstration for one of his classes. He was trying to show that electricity and magnetism were unrelated. Quite by accident he brought a compass needle close to a wire that was carrying an electric current. Suddenly, he saw something that surprised him—something he could not explain and something that scientists had decided could not happen!

INVESTIGATION 30:
OERSTED'S DISCOVERY
To see what surprised Oersted, you will need a magnetic compass, a long piece of insulated wire, several flashlight (D-cell) batteries, paper, rubber bands, and, if possible, some iron filings, wires, and an ammeter.

After stripping the insulation from the ends of the long wire, place it so that it lies parallel to and over the compass needle, as shown in figure 20. Touch the ends of the wire to the opposite poles of a battery so that electric current will flow in the wire. **Don't connect the wire to the battery for long, or you will wear out the battery.** You can make the battery from D-cells (flashlight batteries) in series, as shown in the drawing, or you can use a 6-volt dry cell battery. What happens to the compass needle when current flows in the wire?

You've just seen what Oersted saw. Why was he surprised by this observation?

Repeat the experiment, but this time put the wire under the compass (still parallel to the needle). What is different when a current flows this time? What happens to the direction the compass needle turns if you reverse the connections to the

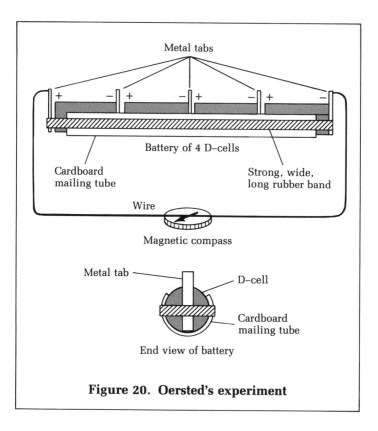

Metal tabs

+ − + − + − + −

Battery of 4 D–cells

Cardboard
mailing tube

Strong, wide,
long rubber band

Wire

Magnetic compass

Metal tab — — D–cell

— Cardboard
mailing tube

End view of battery

Figure 20. Oersted's experiment

battery so that current flows in the opposite direction?

Quite likely, others had made the same accidental observation as Oersted and had paid it no heed. As the French chemist Louis Pasteur (1822–1895) remarked decades later, "Accident favors the prepared mind." Since Oersted was interested in the similarities between electricity and magnetism, he was prepared to take note of the effect that he discovered quite by accident. It was the first clear evidence that magnetism and electricity were related.

CHALLENGES FROM OERSTED

1.   In summarizing the results of a continuation of the experiment you did above, Oersted wrote:

> The effects of the . . . wire (the magnetic field produced by the moving charge) pass through glass, metal, wood, water, resin . . . for if a plate of glass, metal, or wood be interposed, they [the magnetic effects] are by no means destroyed. . . . The effects, therefore, are as different as possible from the effects of one electric force on another.

Repeat Oersted's experiment, but this time place a sheet of glass, metal, or wood between the wire and the compass needle. Do your results confirm Oersted's findings?

2.   To see the shape of the magnetic field around a wire carrying moving charges, arrange the long, insulated wire so that it runs vertically through the center of a white piece of paper resting on a sheet of cardborad, as shown in figure 21. You can support the cardboard on the backs of two chairs.

Move a compass slowly around the wire. You will see that the compass needle always points in the same northerly direction—the direction of the earth's magnetic field where you live. Now connect the ends of the wire to the opposite poles of a 6-volt battery (four D-cells in series). Then move the compass around the wire again. What do you notice about the direction of the magnetic field around the current in the wire? **To avoid wearing out the battery, do this experiment as rapidly as**

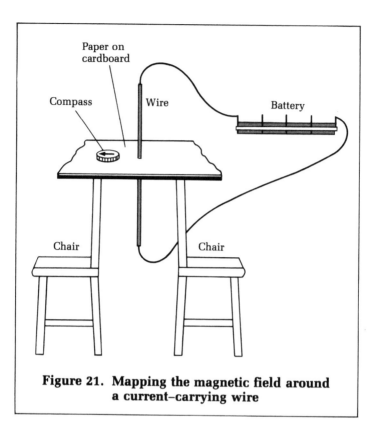

Figure 21. Mapping the magnetic field around a current-carrying wire

possible. **Be sure to disconnect the wire from the battery when you are through.**

3.   Iron filings behave like small compass needles. (You can make some by cutting a roll of fine steel wool into tiny pieces.) Sprinkle some filings on the paper around the wire. Then connect the wire to the battery so that current flows through the vertical wire. Tap the paper and you will see that the filings make a circular pattern around the current.

As you have seen, Oersted discovered that

there is a magnetic field around an electric current. But the field exists only when electric charges are *moving*. If the charges stop moving, as when a wire is disconnected from a battery, the magnetic field disappears.

GEORG SIMON OHM (1787–1854)

During the 1820s Georg Ohm, a German physicist, made a careful study of the relationship between the potential difference (voltage) across a wire and the current (the rate at which charge flows) through the wire. He published the results of his work in 1827. You can repeat his investigation using far more sophisticated meters than were available to him.

INVESTIGATION 31:
OHM'S LAW
To do this experiment, you can use ready-made resistors in which the wire has been carefully wound within a small volume. Obtain a 10-ohm resistor, an ammeter with a range of 0 to 1.0 ampere, a voltmeter with a 0 to 12-volt range, eight D-cells that you arranged in series for Oersted's experiment in Investigation 30 (shown in figure 20), water in a small insulated cup, and connecting wires. Set up the circuit shown in figure 22. Because the voltmeter transmits very little current, you should be sure it is wired in parallel with the resistor, as shown in the drawing.

To maintain a constant temperature, the resistor is immersed in water. Ohm realized that temperature might affect the results.

You can vary the potential difference across the resistor by connecting the leads from the bat-

German physicist Georg Simon Ohm
(1787–1854) discovered the exact relation
between current, resistance, and voltage,
known today as Ohm's law.

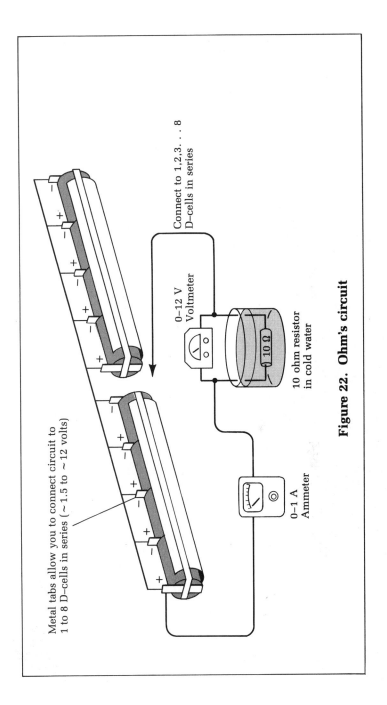

Metal tabs allow you to connect circuit to
1 to 8 D-cells in series (~1.5 to ~12 volts)

Connect to 1,2,3. . . 8
D-cells in series

0–12 V
Voltmeter

10 Ω

10 ohm resistor
in cold water

0–1 A
Ammeter

Figure 22. Ohm's circuit

tery to the resistor to first one D-cell, then two, until you have all eight cells in series. Record the current, in amperes, through the resistor and the potential difference, in volts, across the resistor for each case (one cell, two cells, etc.). To preserve the electric cells and to keep the temperature of the water as constant as possible, disconnect the circuit when you are not making readings.

Plot a graph of the potential difference as a function of the current. What relationship do you find between the current and the voltage? Ohm made the same discovery. After repeated experiments the relationship became known as Ohm's law. State Ohm's law in your own words.

After Ohm's initial work was accepted, the potential difference across a wire divided by the current through it came to be known as resistance and a unit for resistance, the ohm, was introduced later in honor of Georg Ohm. (Of course, an ohm can also be expressed as a volt per ampere.)

CHALLENGES FROM OHM

1. How is the resistance of a particular kind of wire affected by its length? By its diameter? Design and conduct experiments to find out. **For safety reasons, use only DC voltages and do not use voltages in excess of 6 volts.**

2. Do different kinds of wire of the same length and diameter at the same temperature have different resistances? For example, does copper wire have a different resistance than nichrome wire? Carry out experiments to answer this question. **For safety reasons, use only DC voltages and do not use voltages in excess of 6 volts.**

MICHAEL FARADAY (1791–1867)

Once Oersted had demonstrated that a magnetic field was produced whenever electric charge moved through a wire, scientists began to wonder if it might be possible to reverse the procedure and generate electricity from magnets. It was an English scientist, Michael Faraday, in 1831 who first accomplished this—in a way that neither Faraday nor anyone else had anticipated.

Ten years earlier, on Christmas day, Faraday had discovered that a wire carrying current perpendicular to the direction of a magnetic field experienced a force that was perpendicular to both the direction of the current and the field. Faraday used this knowledge to build the world's first electric motor. It was simple and toylike, but it worked.

Faraday was not an educated man and lacked the mathematical facility of most scientists of his time, but, like the great artist and scientist Leonardo da Vinci, he had an uncanny ability to visualize. He regarded magnetic fields as very real "lines of force" that sprang into existence whenever charge flowed in a wire. His keen ability to visualize, together with his brilliant insights, his abilty to design and conduct experiments, and his tenacity, made him one of the great (and perhaps the greatest) scientist of the nineteenth century.

By 1823 Faraday had successfully liquefied a number of gases (including carbon dioxide, hydrogen sulfide, and chlorine) by compressing and cooling them to temperatures well below $0°F$. Previously scientists believed zero was the lowest temperature that could be attained in the laboratory. In 1825 Faraday prepared benzene, a sub-

English scientist Michael Faraday
discovered a method of generating
electricity from magnets.

stance that later served as a base for producing a great variety of organic chemicals.

In 1832 he published what came to be known as Faraday's laws of electrolysis. You can share his discovery of the first law of electrolysis by carrying out the following investigation.

INVESTIGATION 32:
THE FIRST LAW OF ELECTROLYSIS
It was Faraday who named the various components of an electrolytic circuit, names that are still used today. In this investigation you can use 2 inch by 4 inch pieces of zinc about 0.02 inch thick as electrodes (the metals to which the leads from the battery are connected). Clean the electrodes thoroughly using steel wool or a clean scouring pad. Mark one of the electrodes "+" (the anode) and the other "−" (the cathode) using small pieces of masking tape on an upper corner of the electrodes. Weigh the electrodes on a sensitive balance (one that will measure mass to at least ± 0.01 gram) and record the mass of each electrode. The electrodes are to be immersed in a solution of zinc sulfate—the electrolyte. You can make the electrolyte by dissolving about 40 grams of hydrated zinc sulfate ($ZnSO_4 \cdot 7 H_2O$) in 200 milliliters of distilled water (or very soft water, such as rain water). Pour the electrolyte into a clean 250-milliliter beaker.

Put the zinc electrodes that you have weighed on opposite sides of the beaker, and support them with clamps of some kind, as shown in figure 23. Connect the electrodes through an ammeter (0 to 1 ampere) to the proper poles [of one of the cells of the battery you used in Investigation 30]. The anode (+) should be connected to

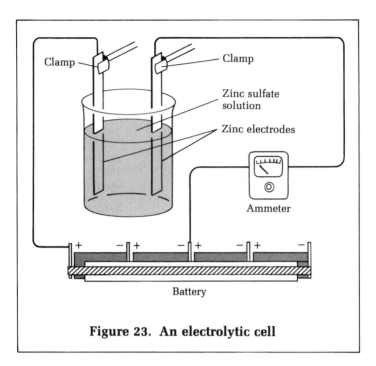

Figure 23. An electrolytic cell

the positive pole of the battery and the cathode
(−) to the negative pole of the same battery. At
the moment you connect the electrodes to the battery, start a stopwatch or record the time. Quickly
increase the number of cells connected to the
electrodes until you obtain a current as close to
1.0 ampere as possible. Record the current every
thirty seconds for a period of ten minutes. At the
end of ten minutes disconnect the electrolytic cell
from the battery. Carefully remove the electrodes,
dip them in a beaker of water to rinse off the electrolyte, and, **under adult supervision, dry them
under a heat lamp or in a warm oven. Be careful
not to let any water drops fall on the lamp.**
Reweigh each electrode and record their masses.

Which electrode gained mass? Which electrode lost mass?

The charge that flowed through the cell can be determined by multiplying the *average* current that flowed during the ten-minute period by the time (600 seconds). Since current measures charge/time, multiplying the current by the time will give you the charge.

(Current $\times$ time $=$ charge because current $= \frac{charge}{time}$, therefore, $\frac{charge}{time} \times$ time $=$ charge)

In this case, since time is measured in seconds and current in amperes, the charge will be in the units *ampere-seconds* (A-s). For example, if the average current was 0.85 A and the time was 600 s, then the charge that flowed was

$$0.85 \text{ A} \times 600 \text{ s} = 510 \text{ A-s}$$

Put the electrodes back in the solution of zinc sulfate and make another ten-minute run repeating all the measurements you made before. Add the charge that flowed in this run to the charge that flowed in the first ten minutes. The mass changes on the electrodes (after drying) will be the sum of both runs, of course.

Continue doing this for ten-minute periods until you have made five or six runs. After each ten-minute run, record the total mass change on each electrode and the total charge that flowed. Then, after you have finished the experiment, you can use all the data you have collected to plot a graph of the mass of zinc deposited on the negative electrode, as a function of the charge that had flowed through the cell. What do you find?

Where do you think the mass that collected on the negative electrode came from? What happened to the mass that was lost from the positive electrode? Based on your data, what do you think Faraday concluded about the relationship between the mass deposited on the cathode and the charge that flowed through the electrolyte.

To see if other elements behave in a similar way, you can repeat the experiment using copper electrodes in copper sulfate and lead electrodes in lead nitrate. You can use 2 inch by 4 inch 20-mesh copper gauze for the copper electrodes and 2 inch by 4 inch lead strips that are about 0.02 inch thick for the lead electrodes.

To prepare the copper sulfate electrolyte, dissolve about 30 grams of hydrated copper sulfate ($CuSO_4 \cdot 5H_2O$) in 200 milliliters of distilled or very soft water. The lead nitrate electrolyte can be made by dissolving 25 grams of lead nitrate ($PbNO_3$) and a pinch of gelatin (gelatin helps the lead adhere to the electrode) in 200 milliliters of distilled or very soft water. Be sure to dispose of the lead nitrate properly; do not pour it down the drain.

The experiment with copper can be done in the same way that you did the zinc experiment. In the case of the lead cell, it's best to measure mass and charge at five-minute intervals for a total of thirty minutes. It's also wise to bend the lead electrodes into convex shapes that face each other, as shown in figure 24. (To see why, try the experiment without bending the electrodes.)

How do your results with copper and lead cells compare with the data and graph you found

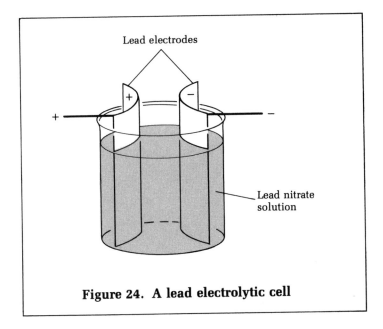

Lead electrodes

+

−

+ −

Lead nitrate
solution

Figure 24. A lead electrolytic cell

for zinc? What do you think Faraday concluded after conducting experiments similar to yours for a large number of elements?

INVESTIGATION 33:
FARADAY'S DISCOVERY
Perhaps Faraday's greatest discovery, in terms of its effect on civilization, occurred in 1831 when he finally succeeded in generating an electric current from magnets. His success, however, was probably accidental to some extent.

Placing very strong magnets near coils of wire had failed to produce any flow of electric charge in the wire. Success came only when the magnetic field moved relative to the coil of wire. Faraday described the experiment that led to his discovery in this way:

Photo of one of
Faraday's electromagnets.

Two hundred and three feet of copper wire in one length were coiled around a large block of wood; another 203 feet of similar wire were interposed as a spiral between the turns of the first coil, and metallic contact everywhere was prevented by twine (that served to insulate the wires). One of these helices was connected with a galvanometer, the other with a battery of 100 pairs of plates 4 inches square.

When the contact was made . . .

To see what happened when contact was made, you can repeat Faraday's experiment. Connect a solenoid (cylindrical coil of wire) to a 12-volt battery or a 12-volt DC power source. (**Ask an adult who understands electricity to help you if you use a power source.**) Connect a second solenoid that will fit into or around the first one to a galvanometer, as shown in figure 25. Notice that this coil is not connected to a battery or any other source of electric current.

Watch the galvanometer when the first coil is connected to the battery. What happens? Watch to see what happens when the battery is disconnected. When does current flow in the second coil? What do you conclude?

Faraday suspected that the effect was the result of a changing magnetic field; consequently, he tried another experiment to test his hypothesis. You can again repeat his experiment. Simply move a strong bar magnet into and out of the coil that is connected to the galvanometer. What do you find? Was Faraday's hypothesis correct? What do you notice about the direction of the cur-

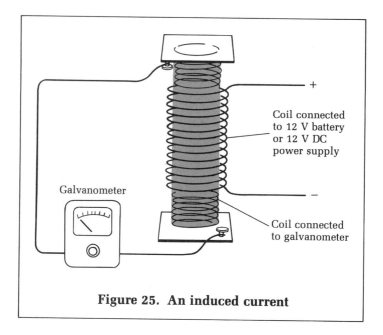

Figure 25. An induced current

rent as the magnet is pushed into and then pulled out of the coil? Does it matter whether the axis of the coil is vertical or horizontal when you do this?

Suppose you hold the magnet in place and move the coil back and forth. Are the results the same?

Faraday concluded that a current is induced (charge is made to move) in a conductor only while the conductor is in relative motion across lines of magnetic force. Do you agree?

Faraday's work led to the realization that by turning a coil of wire in a magnetic field, a continuous flow of charge could be produced. Through the efforts of Thomas Edison, George Westinghouse, and others during the late nineteenth century, Faraday's discovery led to the electrification of the world. To appreciate the significance of Faraday's discovery, all you have to do is to imagine what your life and the world would be like without electric power—without electric lights or electric motors; without electric refrigerators, air conditioners, stoves, and water heaters; without television, radio, stereos, computers, microwave ovens, and thousands of other devices that we take for granted in our electrified world.

Most of the experiments that scientists are working on today require an understanding of the principles that these and other pioneers of science developed. The experiments found in today's laboratories are generally more complex than the ones these early scientists performed, but the methods, the thinking, and the thrill of discovery can be found there still.

FOR FURTHER READING

Andrade, E. N. da C. *Sir Isaac Newton*. New York: Anchor Books, 1954.

Asimov, Isaac. *Asimov's Biographical Encyclopedia of Science and Technology*. New York: Doubleday, 1964.

Bolton, Sarah K. *Famous Men of Science* (4th ed.). New York: Crowell Jr. Books, 1960.

Brown, Bob. *Science Treasures: Let's Repeat the Great Experiments*. New York: Fleet, 1968.

Brown, Sanborn C. *Count Rumford: Physicist Extraordinary*. New York: Anchor, 1962.

Cohen, I. Bernard. *The Birth of a New Physics*. New York: Anchor Books, 1960.

Dunning, Dorothy C. *Experiments in Biology*. Dubuque, Iowa: Kendall Hunt, 1986.

Faraday, Michael. *Faraday's Chemical History of a Candle; Six Illustrated Lectures with Notes and Experiments*. Chicago: Chicago Review Press, 1988.

Feldman, Anthony, and Peter Ford. *Scientists and Inventors*. New York: Facts on File, 1979.

Harre, Rom. *Great Scientific Experiments: Twenty Experiments that Changed Our View of the World*. New York: Oxford University Press, 1983.

Herbert, Don. *Mr. Wizard's Experiments for Young Scientists*. New York: Doubleday, 1959.

Hinds, Conrade. *100 Experiments for Physics*. Dubuque, Iowa: Kendall Hunt, 1987.

Mayer, Jerome. *Boiling Water in a Paper Cup and Other Unbelievables*. New York: Scholastic Inc., 1972.

Shamos, Morris H., ed. *Great Experiments in Physics; Firsthand Accounts from Galileo to Einstein*. New York: Dover, 1959.

Sootin, Harry. *Twelve Pioneers of Science*. New York: Vanguard, 1960.

Stone, George. *Science Projects You Can Do*. Englewood Cliffs, N.J.: Prentice-Hall, 1963.

———. *More Science Experiments You Can Do.* Englewood Cliffs, N.J.: Prentice-Hall, 1981.

Williams, George A., and Richard Barnes. *Physical Science.* New York: McGraw-Hill, 1978.

INDEX

Page numbers in *italics* refer to illustrations.

ABOUT THE AUTHOR

Robert Gardner taught biology, chemistry, physics, and physical science at Salisbury School in Salisbury, Connecticut, for more than 30 years prior to his retirement. Mr. Gardner's books on science for children and young adults have won several awards and citations. His *Science and Sports* (Watts) was selected as an Outstanding Science Trade Book for Children in 1988 by a joint committee of the Children's Book Council and the National Science Teacher's Association. He has also written *Ideas for Science Projects*, *More Ideas for Science Projects*, *Experimenting with Illusions*, and *Experimenting with Inventions* for Franklin Watts. Robert Gardner now lives on Cape Cod with his wife, Natalie.